F*CK

YOUR ANXIETY!

The Art of Getting Rid of Unnecessary Anxieties and Live a Good Life

By

JULIAN CLARKE

TABLE OF CONTENTS

INTRODUCTION

Anxiety seems to come from nowhere for most people, and strike them like a sledgehammer. One minute, living your life more or less peacefully, the next, frightened and depressed, maybe struggling to breathe, convinced you're dying, or someone else is going to die, and it's all going to be your fault. Perhaps you're seeing a doctor right away, maybe you're struggling on your own for as long as you can, but you're going to be told sooner or later that it's Anxiety.

That makes no sense whatsoever. You know what Anxiety really is. It's looking at the clock and uncomfortably asking why someone is late. When parking on a hill, it is double-checking that you put the handbrake on. It is not this living nightmare that turns every minute of each day into a troubling torment. Your natural Anxiety has become out of control and an Anxiety Disorder. Or put it another way, everyone has some fear, but not everyone has Fear. Within this book, we're talking about a disease when we give Anxiety a capital 'A,' and you can heal from that.

Many people use self-help to stage a complete recovery. Others may also need a professional's help to finish their research, but they may go into the sessions armed with self-knowledge and a greater understanding of their illness. Anxiety, that's a black hole. It sucks your dreams, your desires, your expectations for the future, and your strength above all. But it's picky. It lays doubts, worries, and fatigue behind it. It's no wonder you feel like picking up yourself and having the resources for a treatment program. No wonder you're feeling like being in your safe place and doing as little as you can. You can transform this round. It is possible to get back from the Anxiety's dark hole. This book aims to help you set up a self-help rehabilitation plan and obey it. Acting at your own pace, you will learn to let go of Anxiety and recover your life in small measures.

Ways to use this book

You may feel ready to take on the task of working towards a full recovery. The idea may intrigue you, but you're nervous about it. Or you can sense a profound resistance to that. Whatever your current feeling of recovery is, whether you feel hopeful, depressed, or somewhere in between, you can start with this book. You can use the ideas and activities in whatever way currently serves you best, and you can come back to them at a later date when you're ready for further development. There are four different ways this book can help:

1. Relief from the worst forms of Anxiety and improved control of daily life.

You'll learn a set of essential tools to make you feel better, have more power over your life and have more confidence. By learning to relax, exercising more, eating and drinking more sensitively, learning not to be afraid of panic attacks, practicing self-exposure, and transforming negative thoughts to positive, you can feel more able to cope with your life now.

2. Recovering from the latest bout of Anxiety

In this book, there are several different approaches described. When you work through them, you will be developing a full Stress Management portfolio. Not all of them are going to work for everybody, but the only way to find out is to try each. Then you can build your rehabilitation plan.

3. Future problem-solving

Although you're over the worst, failures will happen. Life keeps posing challenges. When you're ready for them, they're not going to overpower you or drive you back to your safe retreat. When you've learned through this book, you'll be given the skills you need to prevent relapses. You're going to be able to identify Anxiety's early warning signs, and you're going to know which strategies work best for you to cope before it takes hold. So if you're facing a loss, you can look at the situation, so ask yourself what you might learn from it and how you could have done it differently. That is more than first aid – these are survival devices and a future that is less vulnerable to Anxiety.

4. Growing as an individual and increasing unused potential, You may feel the need to make changes in your life as you look deeper into the causes of your Anxiety. You can pick how far you're going down the lane. If you're satisfied with

rates 1, 2, or 3, then that's perfect. The main thing is that in your life you will make your own decisions in essential areas – this is a genuinely safe condition. You feel stuck or overwhelmed by it when Fear dominates your life, but when you work through this book, you will start taking control back and begin to live your best life.

This book is intended for use by adults who are struggling with anxiety. With respect to adolescents, while they may have issues displaying many of the same symptoms as adult anxiety disorders, we do not suggest attempting to adopt a self-help strategy without having guidance. Most kids go through stages where they are frightened of certain things – these are part of their natural development and are usually outnumbered. If issues continue far past the expected age or cause significant disruption to the everyday life and relationship building of the child, some professional assistance and advice may be required. It is best to receive a thorough assessment that takes into account the general health of the infant, the overall growth, and any factors that contribute to the family or community.

The various practical steps listed in this book are aimed at making easy for you to deal with anxiety as it concerns your mental health, family life, business, social and other aspects of your life that are draining you mentally and causing you to develop anxiety. Yes, you can beat this and this book is just what you need!

CHAPTER ONE

THE JOURNEY INTO MANAGING ANXIETY

Anxiety is a common emotion everyone will face at various points in our lives. Everybody encounters some type of anxiety on an everyday premise. It tends to be a useful feeling, making you engaged, alert, and productive. However, it can likewise be unbelievably upsetting, awkward, and challenging to live with. In this chapter, I will be explaining the nature, experience, and manifestations of anxiety, show how it can influence your body and psyche and assist you with recognizing whether your levels of stress are severe or ordinary. I will additionally acquaint you with how to manage anxiety, intentionally cultivating calmness, and living a stress-free life daily. Three emotions can cause stress, either good stress or bad stress, and they are Fear, Excitement, and Anxiety. They affect our stress levels in different ways. However, a better understanding of them will help us cultivate better habits to stay calm and enjoy a stress-free life.

The similarity between Fear, Excitement, and Anxiety

Fear, Excitement, and Anxiety are mostly underlying feelings. Every one of the three can generate similar emotions; however, significant contrasts exist between them. Fear and excitement can be useful feelings, whereas stress and anxiety can now and again bring about a great deal of distress. In this chapter, I clarify the contrasts between these three emotions.

What is Fear?

Fear is a characteristic natural feeling, as is anxiety. Indeed, Fear raises similar emotions that nervousness can, for example, alertness or apprehension. The thing that matters is that with Fear, these emotions have a purpose for them. Fear is an inclination of terror, misery, or alert brought about by a threat or danger. For instance, you may feel fear when you see a vehicle racing toward you at high speed. Another example that can trigger anxiety is when you're in a situation where you may slip and fall or at the sight of a snake or any poisonous animal.

The Contrast Between Excitement And Fear.

Various emotions, for example, distress and trauma without a justifiable reason, are one of the primary factors of anxiety. Anxiety is like Fear; however, with no undeniable threat. It's an idea centered on something turning out badly later on and is regularly a thought that things are more than they indeed are. Most times, an awful mishap or loads of stress-causing factors to trigger anxiety, however different the events it doesn't have a recognizable explanation.

Anxiety (stress) is what a lot of people experience, yet the explanation behind it isn't in every case as clear, although it is dissimilar to Fear. Everybody on the planet encounters some degree of anxiety eventually – it's a special part of the human experience! Be that as it may, you're finding your anxiety hard to manage, don't stress: Anxiety can be a truly treatable condition. In the physical sense, excitement is fundamentally the same as anxiety. In case you're charged up for something, you may perceive the same physical sensations, for example, a faster heartbeat and perspiration.

Even though excitement can stimulate indistinguishable physical responses from stress, the only thing that matters is how you feel internally because that is the best place to control it. Feeling excited makes you think positively about the future or past encounters, creating exciting memories, for example, sentiments of joy associated with your physical expression of happiness. In case you're stressed, you might be awakening each day with a similar feeling of fear, yet there may be no genuine explanation behind it.

UNDERSTANDING THE EFFECT OF ANXIETY ON THE MIND

The mind communicates anxiety through worry, a sad expression on the face, and agitation, which regularly evokes a variety of pictures, thoughts, and emotions. One of the principal anxiety issues that individuals experience is uncontrollable, excessive worries over anything, from minor to important things, despite no genuine risk of threat. Your worries can appear like a few kinds of upsetting thoughts and emotions, for example, the accompanying:

- Thinking that you may lose control (go distraught)
- Feeling withdrawn from your general surroundings
- Assuming that everybody is watching your every move which makes you restless
- Wanting to flee to evade the circumstance
- Visiting the Hospital frequently with imagined stress over your wellbeing (for instance, believing that you have a disease or a brain tumor)
- Feeling overly sensitive and hyper-cautious to everything around you.
- Just as worrying, anxiety can likewise influence your psyche in different manners:
- Feeling crabby
- Feeling Fearful
- Lacking the capacity to focus
- Needing consolation desperately
- Feeling dependent
- Feeling discouraged
- Losing certainty

Anxiety is incited by thoughts about Fear instead of impending danger, thus implying that the brain gives the idea is about our perception of things. For instance, you may have gone for an interview just once, yet the brain recollects this event as a sad encounter, which creates anxiety. Others may have likewise encountered similar events past interviews, however, got along nicely at the following ones; their brains didn't give the sad experience a chance to dominate and create anxiety - this is why perception is key in dealing with stress.

WHAT ARE THE PHYSICAL EFFECTS OF ANXIETY ON BODILY FUNCTIONS?

As I showed above, 'Explaining the Difference between anxiety' and excitement, the physical consequences for the body from stress, are like the impacts evoked from Fear or excitement, which includes:

- Faster heart rate
- Rapid breathing
- The urgency to utilize the toilet at regular intervals
- Pins and needles
- Dizziness
- Sweating
- Feeling sick
- Tense muscles (particularly in the chest zone)
- Dry mouth
- Headaches

UNDERSTANDING THE FIGHT-OR-FLIGHT RESPONSE

The fight-or-flight reaction dates back to the times of cavern dwellers and is the body's characteristic response to imminent danger. A Physiologist called Walter B Cannon found in 1915 that animals experienced physical changes when faced with dangers. He found that the increase in blood pressure, secretion of some hormones, and other physical and mental changes prepare the animal for fight or flight.

Humans also experience the reaction to danger. Fight-or-flight is valuable when individuals need to safeguard their families against wild creatures, protect them from burning structures or run from a threat they can't ward off, for example, a natural disaster. Be that as it may, when you're simply doing everyday things, for example, heading off to the shops, driving to work, or taking care of kids, this abrupt release of hormones and physical changes that accompanies it can be hard to manage. The excess hormones that your body secretes aren't required. Accordingly, the diminished carbon dioxide level in your lungs and blood can make you feel dizzy or blackout, making you hyperventilate, which is why you can easily develop anxiety fits.

WHY NEGATIVE THINKING IS A NATURAL HUMAN TRAIT

The human brain is programmed to think negatively as opposed to positive thoughts for one simple reason: Survival Instincts.

If individuals constantly thought positivity, they wouldn't develop a natural threat, and humanity wouldn't have survived! If cavern dwellers had constantly relaxed, making the most of their cavern artworks, and just lived without a care in the world, the possibility is that they might have all been killed and eaten by wild animals within a short time of their existence. Accordingly, the mind is normally wired to think more negatively than positively, and individuals are bound to recollect negative events than positive ones. The brain is likewise extremely brisk at attempting to create patterns, regardless of whether it has little proof. It's your brain's way of shielding you from danger.

Envision that you staggered during a work presentation multiple times – stirring up your notes, spilling your espresso, and, for the most part acting like Mr. Bean. The brain recalls these humiliating occasions and creates a pattern for you, conditioning you to believe that each time you have a work presentation, you'll mess up once more. Or on the other hand, say that you've had two terrible relationships in the past: Your brain would reveal to you that all individuals from the opposite sex are up to no good. Be that as it may, you're never again a cavern occupant. You needn't bother with this example of negative reasoning since the risk is no longer as up and coming as it was a large number of years prior. With no genuine risk of the present threat, these examples can bring about tension. What used to be a saber tooth tiger is currently bound to be a paper-tiger. It's important to discover that people can turn on the pressure reaction by their meditations alone, which can have indistinguishable quantifiable impacts from any compromising stressor in the earth.

IS YOUR ANXIETY NORMAL OR SEVERE?

Anxiety of varying degree influences everybody sooner or later. When all is said in done, anxiety comes in two levels:

- Mild or regularly: For instance, being stressed over an up and coming test, job interview, or a medical examination.
- Severe or excessive: For instance, constant worrying with no genuine reason that seriously influences your life and causes you to experience difficulty recalling the last time you felt relaxed.

HOW DO YOU KNOW YOU ARE SUFFERING FROM CHRONIC ANXIETY?

Chronic anxiety levels can be exceptionally unhelpful, meddling with your day to day life and functional capacity. Here are a few properties of high or chronic anxiety:

- Doesn't have a known reason or just an obscure one
- Very extreme, well past ordinary anxiety
- Lasts any longer than ordinary anxiety, maybe weeks or months
- Has a horrible effect on living, maybe prompting unhealthy and addictive practices, for example, consuming medications or liquor, avoidance or withdrawal as methods for adapting.

At times you can have elevated levels of stress without having an anxiety issue that can be a long haul, for example, Generalized Anxiety Disorder (GAD). This is typical and can be brought about by unpleasant and awful life situations, for example, a separation, switching apartments, the passing of a friend or family member, and other challenging life situations, which can create feelings of anxiety.

ACCEPTING THAT MODERATE ANXIETY CAN BE USEFUL

Moderate anxiety that you don't discover incapacitating can be helpful. Everybody stresses, and as long as it isn't unnecessary, it very well may be something worth being thankful for. Anxiety increases your attention span, which can enhance your performance and productivity.

 If I didn't have any anxiety at all, I'd never get this chapter of the book written! In any case, I realize that I have a deadline approaching, therefore my brain is kicking me without hesitation to start writing and stay in my writing zone. Else, I'd even now be at home relaxing and enjoying some quality time with my family! Here are some different instances of moderate anxiety being useful. It could be just before you begin that public speaking; before you take part in any mind game; before you take a test; and before you turn in a significant bit of work for a promotion test or a work presentation. Your anxiety keeps you centered by enhancing your thought capacity, enabling you to remain productive and take care of business.

CHAPTER TWO

DISCOVERING THE COMMON CAUSES OF ANXIETY

In this chapter, I examined a portion of the most typical causes of anxiety. Albeit no specific school of thought yet clarifies how anxiety emerges in certain grown-ups, yet, hereditary factors, psychological stressors, the environment, and childhood all have a specific influence on triggering anxiety. Indeed, even our daily activities can influence stress levels. Just by implementing a few new habits, you may find a solution to reduced your stress levels, enjoy calm, and making your life somewhat easier and stress-free.

WHAT ARE THE COMMON CAUSES OF ANXIETY?

A wide range of factors can contribute to creating anxiety in humans. You may perceive some of them as connected with your encounters with people or things, and you may not. In some cases, anxiety can show up with no known explanation, and at times you can easily locate its source. Regardless of whether your anxiety has a known reason or not, you can, in any case, apply mindfulness while reading this book in the same way.

As you read this chapter, remember that identifying with any of the encounters I state in this book doesn't mean you're doomed to a lifetime of anxiety holding you to ransom. Anxiety is one of the most widely recognized mental health conditions, and a lot of individuals may have had a portion of similar encounters you've had or are having. The truth of the matter is that you can effectively manage your anxiety. Anxiety, in itself, is a characteristic human feeling that everybody encounters now and again. When I speak about anxiety, I'm talking about continuous feelings of anxiety that negatively affects your productivity, both at work or at home.

DISCOVERING YOUR BIOLOGY AND YOUR ANXIETY

Some studies have shown that anxiety might be hereditary. You may see that others in your close family or extended family have dealt with anxiety at one point or the other. Be that as it may, you can likewise have anxiety when nobody else in your family has ever experienced such. Anxiety is a difficult topic to research because it can likewise be brought about by other external factors that you and your family may know about, for example, troubled homes and Family members, work issues, financial problems, or injury of any sort. Recent studies have shown that if you experience anxiety before the age of 20, close family members, for example, a parent or sibling, are bound to have anxiety too. On account of twins, if one has anxiety issues, the other is bound to develop anxiety issues, sooner or later in life.

In all these, researchers are yet to identify a particular gene that can predispose one to anxiety. Others with similar genetic lineage to you might not have experienced anxiety due to the influence of external factors; for example, their environment might be different from yours.

More research is needed to understand the connection between genetics and anxiety to improve the treatments available for managing stress. Fortunately, your mind and brain can be likened to a book awaiting you to fill in the instruction or answers about how you want it to respond to situations or the best solutions for different triggers. By utilizing the teachings in this book, you can discover the best ways to manage anxiety and also develop the consciousness of living a stress-free life.

DISCOVERING THE STRESS FACTOR

Some types of stress are very normal, based on survival instinct. Everybody needs a tad of worry to keep striving and plan for what's to come. Be that as it may, constant stress, in the long run, predisposes the human body to anxiety. Chronic stress is essentially emotional stress that you suffer for a long time, making you believe you have no control over the situation.

External factors that can prompt chronic stress are:

• Work-related pressure

• Relationship issues

• Family related-pressures

• Financial challenges

• Social expectations

There are several unplanned and planned events that can result in Chronic stress conditions, and sometimes you may not find a tangible reason for it. Internal factors can also cause chronic stress, for example, not getting enough rest, eating unhealthy meals, especially past bedtime, the use of over the counter medications or chronic alcohol addiction can have their consequence on stress.

These practices basically prevent you from having a decent way of dealing with stress or living a stress-free life. When dealing with stress, coping mechanisms are crucially significant when trying to manage stress, and the use of medications and high alcohol concentration in the body discourages such goals preventing such mechanisms from working. You can manage stress by changing your habits and way of life and by utilizing meditation. Little changes, for example, diet, rest, and set aside a few minutes for yourself, can have a major impact on the reduction of stress levels. Be kind to yourself and always bear in mind that you deserve not to be under constant stress – just like every other person around you! Try not to be hesitant to request help if you need it and make an effort not to take on a lot then you can handle in your home and working life.

HOW THINKING CAUSES ANXIETY IN MOST PEOPLE

Most anxiety is generated internally by your thoughts – which doesn't imply that it's your fault! The human mind is easily wired to falling into negative reasoning patterns; it's the mind's way of striking a creative mind about possible negative situations running from itself. Negative or stressful thoughts can result in a reliable stream of unhelpful thought patterns, activated by only one occasion. This habit is called rumination.

Being somewhat stressed, say about your finances, an up and coming test or beginning a new job is perfectly normal; however, if it turns out to be more serious than that, worrying thought can antagonistically influence your life. Mindfulness can help with positive rumination since it trains you to remain in the present time and place rather than fixating on future events. Taking chronic stress as an example, you can see how over-thinking normal events and thought processes can spiral out of control and cause anxiety in individuals.

UNDERSTANDING THE INFLUENCES AFFECTING YOUR ANXIETY

Recognizing any social and emotional factors that might be adding to your anxiety gives you a starting point to apply your mindfulness practice.

Let's Consider The Impact Of Your Childhood Experience

Some Childhood experiencess can add to anxiety conditions in grown-ups. Even though the particular reasons for anxiety aren't known, a connection exists between what occurs in childhood and developing anxiety as a grown-up. If you had a parent with anxiety disorders, for instance, you're bound to experience anxiety yourself. However, regardless of whether that is down to a genetic connection, you exhibiting the anxious behaviors of the grown-up as a kid or a blend of both is as yet indistinct. Other childhood experiences that can cause anxiety are alcohol addiction in the family, child abuse, and excessively critical parenting, excessively protective parenting, suppressing your child's feelings, and separation division from a parent.

A greater amount of these encounters a child is exposed to, the more likelihood of that kid developing an anxiety disorder as a grown-up. Most likely, you can see where the anxiety originates from in a part of these varying childhood experiences. For instance, in the case of an excessively defensive parent, the kid grows up learning fear the world and having the feeling that he can't do anything about it and therefore develops anxiety. On the other hand, for an excessively critical parent, the kid grows up expecting that he can do nothing right and hence develops anxiety. Fortunately, the human brain isn't static and unbendable; you can alter and re-program it. You can unlearn any negative adolescence conditioning with time, practice, and persistence.

Exploring The Self-Observations Effect On Anxiety

Your self-observation – that is, how you see yourself and what you think and feel about yourself – is imperatively important. A lot of people are uninformed of the stream of thoughts that they think in their head each day and the sort of self-talk that they're unintentionally tuning in to.

For instance, do you wind up castigating yourself for seemingly insignificant details that go wrong in your life and blaming yourself for everything? On account of social factors, you may naturally make a hasty judgment about what others consider you. When you're in a social gathering, you accept that they're thinking the most awful of you, passing judgment on your looks, attitudes, clothes, and shoes as though that is the major issue with you.

The thoughts that lead to this sort of negative self-talk aren't accurate, of course. When you become mindful of your thought patterns with mindfulness, you can settle on better choices on the best way to carry on, respond, and gain more confidence.

The vast majority of people are their own worst critics; they don't even give the world a chance to nail them to the cross; they are always feeling pathetic about themselves. This is the worst thing you could do to yourself. You have to acknowledge that just because you see yourself with a specific goal in mind,, that doesn't mean everyone else does, as well. It's simply your warped thoughts that have caused it to appear to be so. (Ever experienced a scene where everyone one particular thing in extremely different ways, for example, while returning from the office with your family, you see a line and there start arguing - 'It's a branch! No, it's a rope! Rubbish, it's a pipe!

You may have heard one of the various versions of an old-fashioned tale around three visually impaired men and an elephant. The first man touches the elephant's trunk, the second, it's the tail and the third its tusk. Each man has a varying encounter of what an elephant resembles because he's touched a unique part. Their unique –varying– encounters imply that they all have a different view of the elephant. Your very own self-recognition is comparably abstract and works similarly.

THE REFUSAL TO IDENTIFY YOURSELF WITH ANXIETY

You may identify with your anxiety by making statements, for example, 'I am on edge or on the other hand,, 'I am an anxious individual.' You may regularly recognize emotions as part of you rather than part of your experience. However, the truth is, you are not your anxiety; it's just a piece of your experience, similarly to reading this section in this book is a part of your experience. The human body is a vessel wherein thoughts and feelings come and go, becoming either good or bad. You may house them for a brief period; however, they don't have a place with you.

Religions, such as Buddhism, consider this habit of relating to your thoughts connection. They propose that rather you express your emotions as 'I'm with anxiety' as opposed to 'I am restless/anxious.' This is a faster way of staying stress-free, give it a trial!

The issue with considering your anxiety to be a part of you and not simply part of your experience is that you further heighten it. For instance, in case you're going to visit your doctor for a clinical test yet have convinced yourself that you may have a life-threatening health condition even though no proof backings this thought, you are sure to experience a lot of anxiety as though you had a life-threatening condition. In the same way, in case you're sitting on a plane, and you experience some disturbance, and you think 'The plane is going to crash,' you may encounter the same anxious thoughts and emotions as if the plane was going to crash!

ENJOYING THE ADVANTAGES OF SOCIALIZING

Humans are social creatures, and various researches have shown that being social can improve your health and wellbeing. In our world today, individuals have smaller groups of friends. They are frequently surrounded by fewer siblings and extended family, for instance, because, for the most part, individuals have decided to have smaller families.

The disintegration of the network, the breakdown of the more distant family, and the busy lives of nuclear family units have all added to this. Individuals with hardly any companions and restricted social contact, for example, not having a friendship network, my battle with mental health issues, for example, anxiety. They don't have anybody to give emotional on their bad days, an upsetting event, for example, a job loss or death of a loved one. Some studies have shown that ladies experiencing anxiety issues who have had positive social interactions, better access to quality information, help, and emotional support generally was in a better state of mental well-being.

Other studies have likewise shown that ladies with somebody to speak with after encountering an unpleasant situation are far less likely to build up a mental health condition, for example, anxiety and depression. Being social (in the case of bantering with colleagues or taking part in Social gatherings) likewise builds your mind's capacity to process thoughts effectively. Such interactions require more attention from you, listening more than you speak and keeping up a decent memory, and realizing when to answer in discussions. Social connections outside your family circle will, in general, have extra advantages because when you experience anxiety at home, accepting external emotional support is progressively valuable.

ACKNOWLEDGING HOW MODERN-DAY LIVING CAN AFFECT YOUR ANXIETY

Living today in our fast-paced world, with individuals being constantly loaded with information in the form of words and pictures, it becomes harder to pick a side without feeling stressed out. Be that as it may, if you stop to analyze this data, you before long find that some of it is pointless and has no benefit for you. The abuse of certain technology and steady information, for example, watching the news, can cause anxiety. Living in this modern world without using technology feels like the stone age all over, be that as it may. In this book, I recommended practical ways to manage your utilization to reduce stress and improve your health and wellbeing.

PREVENTING NEGATIVE MEDIA FROM INFLUENCING YOUR ANXIETY

You retain a great deal of information every day without acknowledging whether it's negative or positive. A huge number of good deeds happen around the world each day but then go generally unreported and unnoticed: landmark events, for example, scientific breakthroughs and cures for diseases, in addition to heaps of little examples, for example, a community joining forces to accomplish something great.

In November 2013, in San Francisco, the entire city was changed into Gotham City with the goal that an ill young man could satisfy his desire to be Batman for one day! This story was accounted for, yet most great deeds aren't. If you watch the news morning and night and read papers, you can without much of a stretch come to accept that the entire world is negative and a shocking place to live in. Listening to negative media all the time can influence your stress levels since you may begin to fear such dreadful events on the TV happening to you and lay awake worried about them.

If you know you are easily prone to being anxious, maintain a strategic distance from the negative news until you feel a little better. If you can't do that, do whatever it takes not to watch it before starting your day since that sets up your day and the last thing at night since you have to loosen up your body into resting mode. Likewise, quit reading beauty magazines; this is because those ridiculous artificially glamorized pictures in them are unhelpful to self-acceptance and self-love, which is what you need to create as a core factor of dealing with your anxiety. Another choice rather than the mainstream news is to go online to www.TED.com, a not-for-profit association devoted to just facilitating inspirational talks by individuals who are intentionally adding to positivity the world.

LESSENING THE UNFAVOURABLE EFFECT OF TECHNOLOGY ON YOUR ANXIETY

You may cherish your smartphone and surfing the Internet for a considerable length of time and using social media channels such as Facebook and Twitter, yet doing so can cause anxiety and fuel existing anxiety conditions. A few studies have shown that the utilization of social media can increase anxiety for two primary reasons:

- **Social media can make you feel incomplete.**

Your Facebook friends might be posting about their lives, their new houses, spouses, wives, children, occupations and vacation pictures. This constant bombardment makes you always wanting to compare your life to others and feeling that you lack something and 'boring' if you don't level up to the pictures they post on social media, which can cause feelings of anxiety.

- **Social media can isolate you from the world around you.**

The more time you spend at home on social media and surfing the net, the less time you spend going out and enjoying valuable time with friends. You need to drop those electronic devices, smell the fresh air and become truly "social", not hiding behind your keypads and faking smiles. Your relationship with your friends is essential for the periods you may be dealing with anxiety since you need their support and physical connections to get through that phase of your life. Spending a lot of time and energy thinking about your Facebook friends and so forth can worsen social anxiety and increase your inclination to stay isolated from people and the world around you.

Social media can be useful in case you're experiencing anxiety disorders; obviously, as a result of all the numerous incredible and resourceful groups and communities, you can get to join online. Be that as it may, in case you're experiencing anxiety, it's best to reduce your social media online time down to only 30 minutes per day. Everybody puts on social media the picture that they need you to see, not all the awful stuff they may be going through. Consequently, you may want to believe that everybody else has an ideal life aside from you, which isn't true!

Your smartphone can likewise cause anxiety. Having it turned on throughout the day, where anybody can get to you whenever it can be distressing because (like the telephone!) you don't get the opportunity to turn off and you are continually accessible. When a work email comes through, you feel compelled to answer it whether it is day or night. Anxiety is brought about by the pressure of technology on you, when, in fact, it should help mitigate your stress levels.

CHAPTER THREE

ANXIETY DISORDERS

As you work through this book, you'll know more about the various forms of anxiety disorder, and you'll be able to relate treatment concepts to your own situation.

Panic attacks

A panic attack is a sudden, generally short-lived but very powerful burst of anxiety. The surge causes physical sensations, which increase dramatically with the progress of the attack. It is fueled by rapid adrenalin released into the body. These vary from person to person, but doctors use the following list – if you feel four or more of these symptoms within a few seconds then you are likely to have a panic attack:

- Shortness of breath
- Discomfort
- Fast or erratic pulse
- Chest pain
- Muscle tension
- Shaking or trembling
- Numbness
- Extreme sweating
- Dizziness
- Nausea
- Urgent need for g. You're left with feelings of fatigue, shakiness, and perplexity after the attack.

Panic attacks are for many people, the base upon which their anxiety disorder is founded. Life is a matter of doing something to stop yet another panic attack for them. And even other sufferers of anxiety never have, and never will, suffered a panic attack.

Phobias

Phobias accept both fear of something particular and fears which are more abstract but still centered. Agoraphobia and claustrophobia These are both a fear of being trapped and incapable of seeking aid or finding a safe location. We are genuinely a phobias class that can involve open spaces, closed spaces, enclosed areas, lines, lifts, public transport, bridge crossing, hairdresser, restaurants, theaters, and cinemas.

Monophobia

That is the paranoia of being alone.

Verbal phobia

This is another cluster related to others. It is more than just being nervous or self-conscious and can involve speaking, eating, or drinking in public, using public lavatories, cooking food or drinking, or writing while being watched. Social phobics also fear that if they blush, sweat, or stammer, they will give themselves away, and the fear makes it more likely they will.

Basic phobias

These are often referred to as simple phobias, as they focus on one thing only. There are hundreds of these, from thunderstorm fears to injection fears.

Generalized Anxiety Disorder (GAD)

GAD is different from a phobia in that you feel overly nervous but without a clear emphasis. You feel nervous, and you can not relax. You can experience many of the panic attack symptoms but without the climactic rush of panic. They may also be continually preoccupied with something bad happening to someone they care about, and you may believe that your concern keeps these people safe. The intense concern is very distressing and may make you feel out of control and can become crazy. Some people describe a peculiar and terrifying sensation of being 'not quite there,' 'unreal' or 'not fully in my body.' In fact, this is not in itself an anxiety disorder, but it is so frequently stated that it needs to be explained. This occurs when someone breathes in a fast, rapid way, which upsets their system's balance of oxygen and carbon dioxide. It is frightening but not deadly. When you've had anxiety for a long time and believe you know everything it can throw at you, so it can be really frightening if these feelings of unreality grow unexpectedly on top of everything else, you've got to deal with.

Obsessive-compulsive disorder (OCD)

OCD starts with obsessive feelings that are so disturbing you are looking for a way to get rid of it. When you are carrying out compulsive behaviors, that way is that you have OCD. Compulsions will also be repeated several times until it seems as if the idea has been canceled out. Obsessive thoughts also involve dirt and illness or injure someone, either by mistake or by giving way to an impulse. Germ-related thoughts may lead to compulsive hand washing or cleaning. Fear of causing harm can lead to gas taps, electrical connections, or car inspection.

Many compulsions may include hoarding (newspapers, food, or even rubbish) or concern about balance or organizing items in a certain order. Often there is an apparent correlation between the compulsive behavior and the object of the fixation – e.g., dirt and washing – but in other cases, no rational relation appears to exist. Of starters, someone believed they needed to reach every lamp post they went through to avoid anything terrible happening to a family member.

The compulsions are often emotions, rather than acts. Obsessive thoughts about harming others or doing something unethical or taboo can lead to compulsive prayer thoughts to cancel the obsessive thoughts. Compulsions continue to increase with time, and you've got to do a longer routine of more repetitions to reach the same amount of immediate Anxiety reduction. This is frustrating, of course, and so someone with OCD will gradually get to a point where they avoid the items that cause their compulsions to the fullest extent possible. This can mean, for example, that someone with an obsession with cleanliness simply gets very dirty because they can't face the big routine of taking a shower or washing their hair. You may have always been a methodical, precise, and patient person if you have OCD. You may have also had a job leveraging those useful qualities. Your useful qualities transform to OCD when you are under stress.

Understanding the difference between OCD and phobia

Sometimes distinguishing between an OCD and phobia can be challenging. There is a sense of being obsessed with most anxiety sufferers – if you spend all your time worrying about having a panic attack, or finding a spider, or meeting someone on the street, then you're obsessed to some extent. And you could suggest behaviors like constantly checking a spider room, or crossing the road to avoid a meeting, have an element of compulsion on them. But OCD has an extra dimension, which is the relation between the obsessions and the compulsions.

Typically, a person with OCD has a strong sense that they need to carry out their compulsions, or some awful outcome will happen, and they almost always feel like they have to perform their compulsions like a ritual in a certain way. So, if you're afraid of spiders and you're going to need to check every room for them, then you've got a phobia. If you believe you're likely to bring bad luck or damage to yourself or your family by letting a spider be in the house, and if you always search the house the same way each time, then you have OCD. Similarly, somebody who is worried about their home protection may double-check that they have locked the door, while somebody with OCD can check, lock, and unlock repeatedly. In addition to other anxiety disorders, such as social and wellbeing phobias, OCD can also occur.

Post-traumatic stress disorder (PTSD)

Post-traumatic stress disorder (PTSD) is caused by risk/abuse exposure. It is classified as an anxiety disorder, although it is related to past events rather than fears about what might happen in the future. Most people who experience traumatic events such as road/rail/air accidents or violent incidents can expect to have at least some disturbing physical and emotional reactions linked to shock and horror. Those are typically short-lived. Aid from family and friends, usually enough to get them through it, with potential short-term medical support. A few people tend to experience PTSD, where they tend to have intense responses for a long period of time, typically thinking they are re-living the trauma and being unable to regain their normal lives. PTSD needs to be handled properly, and we don't suggest using this book or trying self-help.

CHAPTER FOUR

WHAT BIRTHS ANXIETY?

A person who has his first panic attack may think they have a heart attack. Someone calls an ambulance; they're taken to accident and emergency, and they're told after the usual tests that it's panic. The most common reactions to this news are embarrassment and disbelief, but at least a doctor has seen them and can begin the process of getting to grips with what has happened to them. At the other end of the scale, some people have been living with their illness for years without having it diagnosed properly, without talking about it to anyone and without getting any help.

Quite simply, all need to see a doctor discuss their symptoms and get a diagnosis. There are a couple of physical diseases whose symptoms are just like anxiety, so you need to make sure you don't suffer from one of those. There is no point in reading this book and doing the work we suggest if, for example, you suffer from a thyroid problem which tablets can treat. So, if you haven't seen your doctor yet, the time has come to do so now. Consider taking someone sympathetic with you for support if you're nervous about doing this. If you are housebound, ask for a visit to your home. The important thing to remember is if it turns out you have an anxiety disorder, it's a disease, and it's not your fault, so you don't really have to be embarrassed.

Many people worry that their medical records will always show that they have a problem, and in some way, this will go against them. And yet these issues are extremely common, so thousands of people with similar records need to be living happy and fulfilled lives now. You just don't want to be one of them? What's the Doctor going to do? You should expect the doctor to listen and ask you a few questions about what you have to say. Possibly, he or she would do some basic tests to rule out a physical trigger. If you are considering a blood test and needles are an issue for you, then say so. And if you have to wait for another visit to the blood check, you'll have taken the first moves towards recovery. How do I speak to your doctor? Sometimes people are concerned about the way they describe what they feel. It can help to draw up a list of all the sensations you feel beforehand. If you need to think about an accident, don't think too much about it.

A simple statement will start the discussion, and the doctor can ask you questions in order to get more details. 'I was standing in the queue on the bank when I suddenly felt terribly sick, my heart began to pound, and I felt like my legs wouldn't support me.' When you need to explain a constant feeling, keep it easy again: 'I feel so weak every morning that I just can't get out of bed and get worse as the day goes on.' 'I also have to check that the smoke detector works, I know it works, but still, I can't get out of bed.' It can take me to get through it all morning. 'Note these remarks are just to get you going. You do not feel in a position to ask the questions that always bother you: Am I going mad? Is my heart going to stop beating? No matter. You've just made a start.

- And while we're at the subject, let's answer these two questions. A person with anxiety doesn't get mad, and neither anxiety nor panic will make anybody stop beating their heart. What happens next? There are various things that the doctor may say to help you:

- Let's wait and see: if your anxiety is really fresh, waiting for a few weeks to see if it subsides might be a good idea. Use the time to give yourself some TLC and make the improvements we recommend in Part One if that is suggested.

- A short course of tranquilizers: while doctors now agree that tranquilizers are addictive if they are used for too long, taking them for a short period might get someone over a bad patch.

- Other medicines: attempting beta-blockers or antidepressants may be needed. You might need to try more than one antidepressant often to find the best one for you.

- Advice: many surgeries have a nurse who can speak to the patients. Expect to wait for a rendezvous.

- A nurse in mental health: some facilities include a Community Psychiatric Nurse (CPN) who can communicate with patients.

- Mental health unit referral: your doctor may agree to refer you to a specialist in a hospital, but the waiting lists can be very long. Would you worried when you see the words 'mental health'? Anxiety is a mental health concern, but mental wellbeing is a concept that encompasses a wide array of issues, and only a few of them are lasting long-term problems. If counseling is provided to you, cognitive behavior counseling is one of the most popular strategies. Helping people with Anxiety is really popular, and this book is based on its methods, and you'll learn more about it as you move through the book.

Anxiety

It may also make you feel nervous about the word itself. If the figures are right, at some stage in our adult lives, 20-30 percent of the population suffers from some form of anxiety. This is almost 20 million people wandering around, feeling ill at ease at some point in time. Although some degree of anxiety about life circumstances is natural, it is crippling for some people and may turn into full-blown fear or disorders. The quality of life for these people suffers because anxiety disrupts their daily enjoyment of life, their ability to be happy, or even their capacity for success. There are two forms of fear: the normal sensation of discomfort or uneasiness, and phobias or related symptoms.

WHERE DOES IT COME FROM?

The biggest problem-solving the difficulty is that it is often difficult to identify a cause, or even why you feel anxious about it. You can't touch it. It's just a perception that things aren't right, and you're not feeling comfortable or satisfied. Various negative events in life teach many people the world isn't a safe place. These can be traumatic events in their youth, disappointments they've faced, or other problems they've endured. While these events are in the past, they can often cause nervous feelings in the present. In reality, some people use anxiety as a coping mechanism to guard against unpleasant experiences. Being optimistic and feeling good leads to disappointment, so it's easier to feel nervous and enthusiastic and get ready! Nearly everybody in their life has some unpleasant experiences, traumas, or letdowns. Nearly everybody in their life has some unpleasant experiences, traumas, or letdowns. Those who have more than their fair share may assume life is simply not a safe place. They live with a feeling of frustration. Let's learn a bit more about what it is before we take up the solution for this fear. We will also help you recognize which kind of anxiety you are suffering from.

"The "Blahs"

Most people suffer from a widely referred to as "the blahs" daily type of anxiety, which can be hard to identify because it is often not related to a particular event or circumstance. It is always there instead. People with anxiety and fear often associate anxiety with terror, but in fact, they are different. Fear is a reaction to negative stimuli: a risky situation you're about to face, or the fear you won't pass a significant exam that's coming up. In particular, there is something you feel frightened about. Fear is useful, as it motivates you to act — if you see an oncoming car descending on you, fear motivates you to leap out of your way. Everyday anxiety is that feeling that something is wrong is free-floating. You can't really put your finger on it, but it just doesn't seem right to the universe, your life, or your feelings. What exactly is wrong with me? You don't think so.

Why are all the others happy, and I feel so blah? You might feel like "there's going to be something bad" or that there's something you should think about without knowing exactly what it is. You are waiting for the other shoe to drop because not even the first one has dropped yet! If you suffer from anxiety daily, you will rarely feel happiness. Life just doesn't seem amusing, because, at the back of your mind, there is still something nagging. Even when things aren't entirely terrible, there's a residual feeling of the mind. Also, when things aren't overtly awful, there's a residual feeling that the world's just wrong. Anxiety every day can steal your mental health, emotional confidence, and physical well-being. It can cause sleeplessness, lack of appetite, overeating, low-grade depression, and a range of physical ailments, such as stomach upset, headaches, or nervous tics.

Most people secretly suffer from anxiety. They are afraid to admit how scared they are or how nervous they are. The anxiety condition is commoner than we would think. According to the National Institute of Mental Health (NIMH), there is an anxiety disorder in approximately 40 million American adults aged eighteen and older, or about 18.1 percent of those in this age group, in a given year.

CHAPTER FIVE

WHAT DO YOU SAY IN THE FACE OF ANXIETY?

You will recognize the principal areas of your negative self-talk in this chapter. You may find they change over time — your work may be going well right now, but for you, personal relationships are more of an issue. Or you've just been fired from your job, but supports your family. If I asked you if you'd like to speak to yourself about things that make you feel bad, you'd most likely respond, "No." That's understandable: most people don't like being scolded or spoken to, and few people excel in situations where they're constantly reminded of how terrible things are!

You probably don't want to experience the negativity that consumes your mind, but you may not realize it's there — and this is a very important point. It can be so familiar it feels needed and welcome. Earlier, we reported self-talk is stealthy. You feel confident and enthusiastic about your day for one minute, and the next, you're filled with fear and anxiety about what you're going to be facing. Perhaps you might be a little sad for one minute, and the next minute you find yourself shouting at your child, perhaps screaming obscenities at the driver who was edging in traffic in front of you. The transformation is so sly you don't know you have allowed negative self-talking to take over. This is where the tests come in in this chapter.

ASSESSING THE NEGATIVE SELF-TALK

You might be thinking right now, "I'm nervous, but I'm not talking about it to myself. That's what mad people do. "Most people don't wander around in their head, worrying about the sounds. And yet we know that they're here. The first significant move on the path we are going to take together is to discover the root of your negative self-talk. You want to see where it comes from, and you want to know what those voices are saying. This exercise will help you find some of your negative self-talk outlets and see if they're visiting you. When you have some time to sit quietly and answer the questions, complete this segment. You'll need time to think, and then you'll need to be aware of what you're doing every day to capture enough information to work with what you're doing every day to capture enough information to work with as you finish this book. Check out the list of twenty life experiences below. Score about how nervous the will of the following in your journal makes you, in general. Using a 1–10 Scale. One is "Not at all nervous about this"; 10 is "Highly worried and upset about it."

1. Everyday things like being stuck in traffic or burning the toast
2. My place of employment
3. My Employer
4. My family (mom, dad, siblings, and stepfamily)
5. My spouse
6. My boy or kids
7. My Home Life.
8. My Mental Health.
9. My preferred physical fitness, the norm
10. Thinking about my future health
11. My Financial Status
12. My living conditions
13. In my 14th career, caring for others. The list of my things to do.
14. I have made commitments, or somebody's going to ask me to make
15. The Economy
16. External activities, such as social or economic factors.
17. What will happen tomorrow?
18. Reflecting on my professional future.
19. Which has already happened — today, yesterday, or to the past
20. Regrets for my mistakes or things I've done.
21. Guilt for the way I now live my life
22. Now review the list of my feelings of "self" and self-worth.

Circle certain things to identify your nervous reaction for which you choose a six or greater. Copy the example of the worksheet below in your text, and describe the first thing that comes to mind while reading the paragraph. For example, if you choose an eight on, "I've made commitments, or somebody's going to expect me to make," you might write, "Too many people want anything from me. I don't have time to do something I'm supposed to do. "Or, if you choose" My family of origin "on a scale of 9 or 10, you could write," Anyone who grew up with two alcoholic parents will test the scale of 9 or 10.

Isn't it clear how this was anxiety-inducing for me? "Your subconscious is telling you something about the subject you've been swimming around. When you circled a number greater than 5, you thought, "Yes, this is anxiety-inducing for me." It's important what you write about what you think, feel, or say to yourself about this subject. Now go back and re-read what you wrote. These subjects, and what you say about them to yourself, will give you some insight into how negative self-talk slips into your patterns of thinking.

Card Analysis

Write the subjects from the list of twenty items in the above exercise as an extra exercise on separate 3 "/ 5" index cards or a small sheet of paper that you can hold close by while you go about your day. You may have an index card at the top of it, which says "my family of origin." Write down the negative self-talk you find yourself using when you experience circumstances or thoughts about the subject. And be as precise as possible. If you do this regularly, say every two to three weeks, you will have a filled index card with several negative statements about the topic that you make to yourself. If you fill in one card or sheet of statements about this topic, you make to yourself. If you have one card or sheet of paper filled in, take another. Keep adding to it until you get a better and clearer understanding of exactly what you're thinking in response to the issue or the situation. Remember the awareness is a significant first step. Before you can use constructive self-talk to introduce new strategies, you need to be mindful of the sly negative self-talk that comes in and steals from you. Hold these cards close by while you carry on book exercises. Knowing just how you respond and the negative self-talk you use helps you to better understand it and cope more positively and efficiently with it.

Anxiety and Its Effects

Now that we have an understanding of the main causes of anxiety, it's time to look at how you respond to them and the effect on you of the resulting negative self-talk. It is like getting an early warning system to know how the negative self-talk impacts you. If you know there's a tornado coming; you're going to search for cover or go somewhere dry. In the same way, to support you and keep you comfortable, you want to turn on your constructive self-talk. The next segment will allow you to take the time to observe your responses to stressful circumstances and your behavior. You must understand how things are unfolding for you. You can still learn about their anxieties by talking to others, but to bring about the change, you need to know your impacts.

Get Precise

You might not be feeling anxiety at the moment and feel like things are "okay." Though I encourage you to continue reading, you can keep the book handy and pick it up when you're nervous about something so you can document the details. From this book, you will learn many things, but the most important ones will be the most basic for you. Some people don't take responsibility for their lives, so they're not really sure what to do. Their mind is fraught with fear and negative self-talk by the time anxiety has taken over — a runaway train that no one can stop. To stop the train, you want to pull the levers long before it gets to a final crash. Think about the effect that anxiety has on you. For example, if you say you get headaches when you're stressed, are they making it difficult for you to get through your day? Is it the Cumulative Effect? You skip work due to bad headaches, but instead, the missed sick day causes more tension and headache.

Through this review, you can describe how the negative self-talk, or nervous response to the circumstances of your life, is manifesting. Impact learning helps define what is generally considered stimuli, which we will address later in this chapter. Anxiety works directly on you. This may be mental (worry, faulty thought, lack of confidence, lack of life enjoyment) or physical (stomachache, sweaty palms, or tense muscles and headaches); Whatever the signs, the effect is something. It is important to understand how you are affected by anxiety so that you can use your mind and body to alert you to its start. When you learn to decipher the effect of anxiety on you, you are also able to go back and find its source. You will alter your self-talk until you find the source.

CHAPTER SIX

CAPTURING THE NEGATIVITY THEMES

Do you consider any patterns while reading at the list of circled negative words? Of course, alongside all, you might have derogatory words written. You can have derogatory words written next to everything, people course. Those who are diagnosed with anxiety, or who live with a general feeling that all the time something is wrong, will find their responses to most living situations a negative reaction. But there are themes on the list mostly you will find. Perhaps all of your negative remarks were about your life relationships. Perhaps they'd been about wellness. See how the responses are divided into themes. Using the function of your journal or notes to capture these themes. Holding those concepts in mind as the evaluation process continues. If you have defined different areas, concentrate your attention on those chapters that suit your needs most closely. When you get a general feeling of "Life stinks and makes me depressed all the time," you will find that it is necessary to go through each chapter and learn strategies to implement constructive self-talk. Assessing Trigger Responses When the trigger occurs, it is accompanied by a response. Recognizing how your triggers affect you is critical. Often it helps to go mentally through the incident or situation that has caused you — starting from the stage where you feel the anxiety symptoms.

The Unseen Cycle

Everything you witness in life — large or tiny is defined by your perception. Rather than seeing it as what it is — an objective experience — you view it by negative self-talk. Your self-talk gives the situation sense and "color." You concentrate on the negative factors, focus on them, and envision all manner of complicated outcome scenarios. You're going through the process until you're too frightened, confused, and anxious to think clearly about how to stop it. The trick is to either interrupt the loop at the point where a stimulus is about to set it off or when the negative self-talk begins. It's off, or you continue the negative self-talk.

Going Positive

The good news is that another way exists: to practice constructive self-talk. What kind of self-talk keeps you focused and optimistic. This can act as a trigger in many life conditions to help you deal with whatever challenges come your way. It will at least give you energy, rest your fatigued mind, and develop confidence that things are probably better than you thought they were!

Identifying the Voices

Sometimes you will understand their source when you think about what the voices are saying to you. You can learn an ex-girlfriend or boyfriend from your father or mother, or your older sibling, or a former boss. The phrases you use to express something about yourself may be common words that others have used either for themselves or for you. Through the years, those theories have had a tremendous influence on you. When you get attuned to the voices and what they mean, some common themes can come up. Many times people's understanding of what's "good" or what's "evil" is just the viewpoint of someone else who's gotten entrenched. Much as the secret to negative self-talk is to find constructive self-talk, so you can fan your memory's flames to remind you of healthy, optimistic things people have told you.

"Batter them up! "

You will have a chance to complete life-specific evaluations and reactions in the next chapter. But first, let's look in more depth at the difference between positive and negative self-talk and see how it really tells a story in your life. Think about listening to a broadcaster broadcasting a baseball game on a ballpark. Now imagine the announcer really hasn't seen the game yet. He tells the audience what is going on before the play begins. "The next batter up hits a home run. The crowd will go crazy. The batter runs around the bases and is feeling a hamstring. He'll wonder if he should finish without falling down. This would be a wonderful thing to watch! "If you were in the crowd, how much fun would this be for you? Want to know what will happen before it happened? Most people would reply: "No! "The pleasure, watching the game unfold, is in anticipation. The joy of not knowing how things are going to work out. Curiously enough, however, you live your life through your self-talk — whether good or bad — as though an announcer in your head tells the plays before they happen.

You tell yourself what things mean, what will happen next, what is implied by someone's mannerisms and facial expressions, whether the day will be good or bad, and on and on. You don't just have the chance to experience life, because the commentary tells you what the experience is before you get it! Writing the image of the story as well as you can. It is a nice day. You leave your house, and you smell the spring breeze. This morning, you had time to get ready, so you didn't get rushed, and you feel fine. You smile as you walk down the front stairs. Your spirits are up, and they look like a good day is coming. Just as you step on the last step, there comes a man running full force ahead around the corner. He appears to be looking at you straight. As he runs, his long coat flaps behind him, and his face shows what you interpret to be some concern. Keep on here. It's likely that negative self-talk will tell you to be frightened or paranoid. Maybe you have had a bad encounter with a stranger somewhere in the past. You may have been assaulted or mugged by someone you encountered on the street.

Therefore your mind whispered, "Is this guy a threat to me? Maybe he'll catch me or injure me. "Some kind of negative self-talk comes from the situation as well as from the memories of similar circumstances. Yet you needn't give it in. Tap on your optimistic self-talk instead: "Wow, that guy is going really fast. I wish I could be riding like this. I'm personally so glad last week that I started the workout schedule. When thinking about how he's when shape, I just found that I felt a lot better about myself. I think I am really being toned up. I'll consider a couple more opportunities to get more exercise on my calendar. If I do, I just feel so good. He makes me laugh with that cute smile that he's got. When I run to get in shape, I always have a similar phrase. "Which is the" true "story? What story is right, then? Is that guy a threat? Is he abusing you? Or is he a reminder of things you love and care about? You can only answer those questions. Yet you generate less tension and more possibilities for yourself by turning away from the negative to the constructive self-talk.

Want to change?

It's time to learn how to stop and more positively move your self-talk. Self-talk can be used to relax your nervous mind. It is about choices. You haven't had a choice till now — negative self-talk rules your day. Yet it's about shifting. You've done a variety of tests earlier to determine the key causes of anxiety in your life. In the following chapters, you'll learn how to apply constructive self-talk in a variety of circumstances. Learning positive self-talk and saying the right words does not change Practicing positive self-talk by itself, and saying the right words does not change your life overnight. The more you will practice it, however, and make it a routine, the more choices you will have. So the more you will try to substitute negative self-talk with positive self-talk, the more power you can have over your life. Positive self-talk builds up confidence and offers hope.

CHAPTER SEVEN

BUILDING THE SELF-TALK TOOLBOX

Are you about to get a little calmer? Are you ready for the steps you need to take to quench your fear, relax your mind, and make yourself more healthy life-long choices and results? Everything really belongs to you. It feels like these things are out of your control, but inside you is the power. You know it made you more nervous. Yet, it made promises that it can not keep. It's been telling you stories and giving you ends, without ever allowing you to produce a different outcome. The benefit of positive self-talk is that during moments of daily anxiety and tension, even when things get out of control, you can call it on.

The truth is, you are calmer. There's you inside the tornado that can stand while it swirls around you and not get caught in the wind. When you're ready to change a life and prefer calm over nervous, it's time to uninvite the negative self-talk and welcome you into a more optimistic and strong self. Take the steps outlined in this book, learn more about your patterns of negative self-talk, and investigate the integrity of what these voices tell you are all vital pieces of the puzzle. Nevertheless, you need to take a few steps. You need to devote yourself to a new way of being. You've got to decide it's time to allow you to emerge calmer.

Using Your Materials and Assessments

This book is not intended to be a one-time read. It's intended to push you to behave. This book is not intended as a one-time read. It's intended to motivate you to act, and to give you measures, strategies, and ways to push your negative states to something positive. You would think this environment does not require a calm mind and yet many people are standing still in the middle of the tornado and watching it move by. You can do the same. You'll learn in this chapter which strategies you need to keep in your positive self-talk toolbox to keep you relaxed and in charge.

Promise

First of all, is committing yourself. Commit to a new strategy to a new you. Write your dedication to a 3 "upper 5" card or you can post it anywhere and see it frequently. Write it down in the current tense, and sometimes revisit it. You could write something like: "I commit to a calmer me." Or "I'm getting calmer every day." Or "I'm taking the measures I need to take to eradicate negative self-talk from my life." Resolve how you'll catch and define your negative self-talk all day long. What system do you use to keep track of that?

Your Personal Plan

It's crucial to consider the areas of life that you see as big triggers. Although most of life can regularly pose challenges, some places are more stress- and anxiety-inducing than others. To some people, their work-life is fantastic, but they haven't met the person of their dreams, and when they get home feeling depressed and unwanted, they indulge in negative self-talk. Some see fear as permeating everything they do. Others have a bad boss or employment situation — or can't find a job at all — and feel gloomy and discouraged anytime they think about jobs. Just note, once you know what the problem is, you can't fix the problem. There are no correct or wrong responses in the tests. This is all about learning more about your anxiety and yourself. Ignoring what is bothering you, or believing it will go down on its own, is no benefit. And, while this book will offer several guideposts for coping with anxiety and making different decisions, you must first understand where the anxiety comes from, what causes it, and what brings it into motion. Then, you want to be conscious of how it takes over, what it tells you, and how it affects your mind and your body.

Keeping Track of Your Negative Self-Talk

Earlier, I spoke about using 3 "as well as 5" cards to write down negative self-talk so you could know how amok runs and how to combat it. I recommend you get a journal and write down stuff as well. Some people hesitate to do this, but it's incredibly beneficial. When you don't want to keep a journal, try sending a text message to yourself or keeping a note on your smartphone. Perhaps you may want to write down ideas on sticky notes, then post them so you can check them. Consider speaking in a tiny tape recorder that you are bringing with you when something happens to you that will help you recall. Whatever you want to do, you must continue to keep an eye on the negative self-talk and expose it. The more clearly you can see where and where it is creeping in, the more leverage you need to ask it to quit and replace it with constructive self-talk.

Simply using positive affirmations can be helpful, but you have to recognize the negative self-talk and make specific decisions about it to really move from anxiety to a calmer one. Solve here how you'll catch and define your negative self-talk during the day. What system do you use to keep track of that? Take note of the things that cause you, and write down your response to them any time you experience creeping negative self-talk. And don't encourage your notes to sit down any time you find the negative self-talk creeps in. Just don't let unremembered notes lie down. Return to them at least once a day to start seeing whether trends or commonalities exist.

The Next Steps

In addition to writing your dedication to making the change you want and defining a way to keep track and become more mindful of your self-talk, you'll want to consider which parts of this book may be more helpful for your immediate problems. Having looked at the table of contents again, search quickly to find the chapters that most appeal to you. Then, carefully read them. Find the steps that seem ideally suited to your situation, lifestyle, and needs. Copying these pages can be helpful so that you always have them handy. Without a strategy, no real change can happen. You have to find a way to incorporate what you're learning here into your daily life, or it can't be true for you. Study the steps that you are going to take next time negative self-talk is creeping in. Write them down and hold them somewhere you can quickly touch. You might be able to have a package next to your bed so that you can repeat encouraging statements before bedtime. Hold the package in your office pocket or desk drawer. Don't put them in a file — forget about them is too fast. When you need them, put them anywhere you can touch.

First, arrange some time for the mechanism you have defined to work out. Many of the strategies in this book demand that you remain still, breathe deeply, or repeat affirmations. This can be done at any time. In reality, you can practice, so when the negative self-talk visits and you catch it in the act, these exercises become a routine to you! You want to be prepared to return to your constructive approach. The more you do this, and the more you feel relaxed with it, the easier it is to do it. As you read each of the chapters below, put the exercises and As you read each of the chapters below, bring the exercises and guidelines into your proverbial trick bag. Choose which strategies work for you. If you're looking for a friend, find out a way to do this. Getting another person support in turning your self-talk around can be very helpful. When you are doing self-hypnosis, plan that into your day. Do not wait for the right time to make something happen—planning for it instead. Consider it a part of a lifetime. Get it down in writing once you have your strategy. If you have a notebook for preparation, using calendar apps, or put everything in a smartphone, don't rely on memory alone to remind you of the time to do a self-talk exercise! Plan it out. Write them down. Commit to doing so. Without concerted acts, reform does not happen to make it happen.

Review, Modify, and Performance

Instead of thinking everything is going to work well now that you have a strategy, take deliberate action to evaluate what is going on. Not all work for every single person. Any of the solutions may be perfect for your buddy or a friend reading this book, but may not work for you. The reason that this book is filled with ideas and solutions is to give you the opportunity to find the one that suits you. When you practice the methods, be careful what is and what is not. Once, taking some notes and recording the thoughts may be helpful. Just take a note of what it feels like every time you practice it. What didn't fit too well? What was your favorite? What would you like to change next time? Make this cycle about you — do not care about the wrong and the right.

Concentrate on what works for you.

Be sure to catch the "Why? "Why did the solution not work as well as you would have hoped? How has one strategy worked better than the next? What kinds of stuff affected the outcome? Then take note of what you may want to do differently. What influenced the result? Then take note of what you may want to do differently. Next time what do you change? There are pieces that you can take from one solution and bring in with another? Identify the next best move, lastly. Which stuff are you going to keep on committing to moving forward? Stating your dedication on a scale of 1–10 will help. How dedicated are you to making yourself calmer, more peaceful?

Stay Calm, and You will switch from fear to a happier you.

The negative self-talk you've adopted has made you believe this was not possible. Now, you know there is another way. Could you be cool? You should feel okay about yourself. Your life should feel sweet. Commit yourself to that today. Traverse the steps outlined here. Don't go for shortcuts. You deserve peace. You deserve a life as an ever-present nag, without fear. Today, start walking into a new life.

CHAPTER EIGHT

ANXIETY IN PERSONAL RELATIONSHIPS

Relationships are the secret to our happiness and progress, and the bane of our lives, in many ways. Throughout life, the people closest to us can help and direct us, and they can make our lives absolutely miserable too. Many people have not understood how relationships can be genuinely normal and optimistic. You may look to another person for your happiness, and it makes you unhappy if he doesn't do what you expect. You can blame people around you for the problems you have — your parents didn't provide you with the right support, or your siblings ignored you or your friends betrayed you. There's room for problems everywhere human beings meet. Most people are well-intentioned, but how they act in a relationship is uncomfortable or self-destructive. Harry, for example, craves publicity (a good outcome), so he attempts to gain it by behaving violently and creating scenes in public places (poor delivery). The effect is just the opposite of what he wants — people shun Harry for not being part of his destructive behavior, and as an effect, Harry doesn't get what he really needs. Sometimes it seems as if our relationships always have something amiss. While things go well with your spouse, you may struggle with your neighbor.

If your kids' act, your mother-in-law causes you trouble. The negative self-talk, which is often the third wheel in our relationships, fuels these relationship issues. Negative self-talk affects your response and other people's experience in the circumstances ranging from coping with tension and frustration in relationships to loss of a loved one to life disappointments. This chapter will explore the various types of relationships that trigger tension and anxiety and look at the common people who use self-talk. You'll do some exercises to analyze your own self-talk and learn new constructive approaches from some exercises to analyze your own self-talk to learn new constructive ways of talking to yourself to help repair some of your broken relationships or negative feelings toward others.

Relationships Can Really Hurt.

It's fascinating to study how relationships can really hurt. Negative self-talk and the resulting anxiety may actually cause hurt to one another. Some reports have shown that approximately 50 percent of violent crimes against family members are committed against spouses each year. In the United States, one woman is assaulted or beaten every nine seconds. At least one in three women around the world has been raped, forced into sex, or otherwise violated during her lifetime. The victim is most frequently a part of her own family. Domestic abuse is the leading cause of women's injury — more than a combination of car crashes, muggings, and rapes. A mind that is driven by negative self-talk does not "see" another person as worthy.

Relationship issues

Begin by understanding the vast network of relationships you're interested in. Your family of birth, including your parents and siblings, and any extended family members, including aunts or uncles, are present. You may be dating, divorced, or in a relationship you have committed to. You might have kids. You also have friends and colleagues that you frequently communicate with. And in this social networking era, relationships are pervading our lives. We also spend hours chatting, reading, and learning knowledge about other people online. You do make you happy or hopeful about the world when your relationships are healthy. A good link in the storm of life can be a port. Yet when relationships get unpleasant or face challenges, most people get stuck on the issues and use negative self-talk to drag down themselves and others. Problems and use negative self-talk to get down on themselves and on others.

Too much negative self-talk can turn love or attraction emotions into hate or disgust. In other situations, you are feeling depressed or losing. You could have been through a divorce or lost a loved one. Depression and anxiety are normal, overshadowed by negative emotions. You allow your negative self-talk to take over instead of concentrating on positive self-talk — remembering the good times you've shared with your mate, relative, or spouse. "I'll never get my life full again. The loss is too big — the hole is too big. "Or," I'm too young to be alone, so I'm going to be alone for the rest of my life. "I'm not satisfied, but I don't know how to tell you.

Behavioral research tells us that only about 18 percent of the population is comfortable with conflict. Wherever possible, that leaves 82 percent seeking to avoid conflict; at best, they accept it when it comes to their way. The problem is, partnerships have underlying some degree of conflict. This can be as small as leaving the cap off the toothpaste in the bathroom, or as big as telling your spouse you don't want to have kids when you said you've been open to them before! There are hundreds of chances every day for differences of opinion to emerge in intimate relationships.

But relationships are not limited to romantic ones, of course. There's the sibling at the last family meeting, who acted inappropriately (at least in your view). Or the child that answers your rules with, "I hate you! "Relationships are a daily platform for conflict. Many people are so attuned to the tension that they wait anxiously for the other shoe to drop, even though a relationship is fairly harmonious. You can adopt an attitude of avoiding conflict, hoping that it will resolve itself, but as you have probably learned the hard way, that is not happening. Unresolved disputes boil and bubble just below the surface before they explode. For this reason, being able to deal with conflict in a relationship constructively and positively is a valuable skill.

Changing Your Self-Talk to Deal with Others

We need to combat negative self-talk that can take us off track considering the critical role relationships play in our lives. Here's what it takes you to do.

Phase One

Take the time to consider what you want in this relationship. How would the partnership look like if things went as you would like them to? How does the other person do or say? Why should you communicate with him, or with her? What questions would you like to ask for a positive outcome with that person? Make notes about how you want this relationship to be and how you want to be in that relationship. And be as straightforward about what you really want as you can.

Phase Two

Now take a minute to sit quietly and imagine what it's like to feel comfortable now take a minute to sit quietly and imagine what it's like to feel secure about this relationship, and in a good position. Close your eyes and imagine the good emotions in any way you can be of support. Not everybody in their minds "sees" images, and that is all right. Only imagine how you might feel about the relationship and what you might think about it. Picture what the other person does to you in reaction. Is he more effective at listening? Are you solving issues together? Are you just having fun? Run images, emotions, feelings, or ideas through your mind about your desired positive outcome for this relationship.

Phase three

Practice constructive self-talk now.

Read the following phrases to see the ones you to your situation are better suited to, or the ones you can most relate to and seem the most "true."

"I deserve a good relationship." "Personal relationships are supposed to be rewarding, not exhausting." "It's important to raise problems, questions, feelings, ideas, or whatever I want to talk about in my relationships." Thinking about challenges gives us a chance to resolve them together." "I don't monitor other people's reactions. I can only control my own actions and reactions." "I stay focused on what I want as a result of this relationship, not on what's wrong. I think it can work in that relationship. I'm trying to find new ways of doing my part in that end. "

Phase Four

Now bring all of this together. Find a place to rest and close your eyes quietly. Now bring all of that together. Find a place to rest and close your eyes quietly. Suppose this is a good friendship. Picture it, giving you joy. Imagine that in this relationship, you can be honest and feel good about yourself. Get an idea about the next contact with this person in your mind. See or assume contact would result in a positive outcome. Look at the above list and pick the self-talk to make these pictures real for you. Practice these words and repeat them again and again until they appear to you as real. It's really important for you to let those words sink in. The more that you allow your mind to understand ideas and images and words that make this relationship more meaningful and satisfying, the more it will help you work towards that end.

Phase Five

Be sure to keep your journal or tape recorder close by while you deal with this. Monitor the person in the relationship for your reactions. Note where you get stimulated, and where your constructive self-talk will support. Looking at the cycle as ongoing is crucial so that you can continue to reinforce the new, more constructive approach. No connection will change overnight, note. In relationships, people adopt such attitudes and reactions, and it takes a while to accept new habits on the part of someone you might be close to. You'll need to dedicate yourself to plow through even though your negative self-talk tells you there's no point, and nothing can improve.

CHAPTER NINE

HELPING YOURSELF TO OVERCOME ANXIETY

A degree of self-help involves dealing with most health concerns. Just something as easy as having to recall taking your tablets is self-help. Exercises may be given to someone with a joint injury to practice at home; dietary rules will be given to a diabetic, or lifestyle advice will be given to a heart patient. The self-help element is key in the case of anxiety disorders. If you don't cooperate with them, the best therapist in the world can't help you, and drugs will only dampen the symptoms down to a level where you feel capable of doing the work you need. Every time you speak to a compassionate friend or family member about your problems, you support yourself. Reading around the subject helps you understand your illness. There are self-help groups in certain places where people meet to socialize and give each other support. Finally, there are the telephone helplines run by volunteers who themselves are near all the sufferers. And whatever recovery path you choose, it will require self-help. However, this book gives you a full self-help approach. You can use it completely on your own or with other support in conjunction-but, please tell your therapist that you are using it.

Qualities needed to achieve self-help

- Everyone may apply self-help principles. If your Anxiety is moderate or serious, recent or chronic, it doesn't matter. You should always do anything to launch yourself on the road to recovery. What are your unique qualities?

- Commitment: you might be at the investigation stage of your choices, with the intention of leafing through this book to see how it is. That's good, but it is best to do so with the resolve to give it a reasonable chance when you are ready to start work.

- Time: to work on your recovery, you'll need to set aside some time every single day. The amount of time required varies from person to person, and many of the tasks you do are not going to be too difficult and may even be pleasurable.

- Patience: Anxiety has no miracle cure or invisible wall, and your progress can feel painfully sluggish in the early stages. If you stick to it, you'll find progress is being made, and it's getting easier.

- Motivation: how much would you want your Anxiety Disorder to be free? That's what motivates you, and our research shows that most sufferers have a lot of it.

- Courage: at this moment, you probably don't feel courageous but just sit and think. How difficult is it to face every day realizing that you will have a panic attack, or that your phobia may torment you, or that your OCD will overpower at any moment? Doesn't it take some bravery?

- Help: Sometimes, people don't want to accept that they have an anxiety disorder, but if you can find someone to help you, they'll help you through the hard times.

IF YOU ARE READY TO START YOUR RECOVERY PHASE, ANSWER THESE QUESTIONS

- How committed to recovery, are you too deal with anxiety?
    A bit / quite a lot/100 percent

- How much time do you give the job every day?
    Very little/30 minutes / at least an hour

- Are you ready to wait a while to reveal the results?
    Yes / No

- How do you feel about an Anxiety Disorder?
    Not bothered / fairly unhappy / finding it intolerable

- Are you ready to face up to what is needed?
    Yes / No

- Have you found any positive source?
    Yes / No

Would you like to scream, 'I am dedicated and inspired, of course, just show me what to do?' Good ...... good. When you get angry with us, we don't mind-rage gives you strength, just what you need right now. To many anxiety sufferers, perhaps the hardest thing is just making time for a treatment plan. Most sufferers of anxiety are very busy individuals, in one constant hurry, balancing family obligations, work, and anxiety. Others are kept distracted by their fear-OCD can be very time consuming in particular. At first, finding enough time will be hard, but slowly you'll turn it around, life will be less complicated, and you'll have more time at your fingertips.

CHAPTER TEN

TWO KEY SKILLS: TARGET SETTING AND RELAXATION

Key Skill – Setting target Recovery for getting rid of anxiety is based on setting goals and achieving them. Goals need to be practical. Do you feel impatient? Want to hurry in the first week and do whatever we suggest? You'll have to control the enthusiasm. Taking on a target that's too big for you will lead to disappointment, and you'll feel like abandoning. Make targets only small enough to get you a fair chance to succeed. Are you inclined to be self-protective too? You may need to brace yourself in that situation and take a little more risk. Goals that are too small do not present a challenge, and achieving them brings little reward. Choose clear goals. Don't claim to be happy is my target. Do tell 'my intention is to quit counting my coat hangers' or 'my intention is to post a message.'

Divide targets into small steps.

The solution to each of the above difficulties is to break down targets into small steps. Start by choosing an overarching target, and then see what smaller goals you can set to help you get there. The smaller milestones can also be broken down – below is an example of how to do that.

Keep a goal log and progress.

Use your notebook to document the goals and measures.

Learn from the mistakes

Counselors and therapists believe mistakes are more valuable than successes because they teach us so much. Do not let yourself sink into depression if you fail at one of your goals. Instead, be your own therapist and try to understand why you have suffered – this is the question you have to solve. Rearrange the target, so next time you get a better chance of success.

Repeat the targets

Seek to do more than once on every goal. Eventually, it should become easier each time, though the occasional setback can occur. Example of goal setting – running the marathon We will later provide examples of goal setting for recovery from anxiety, but let's look at an example for now that has nothing to do with anxiety. A very unhealthy person wants to run the marathon in order to raise funds for his favorite. A trainer helps them break their goals down.

Key target Marathon race.

Secondary Objectives

1. Race one mile.

2. Race 5 kilometers.

3. Race 10 km.

4. Half marathon race.

And so on until the marathon's actual day.

Breakdown of the first goal

Because this individual is really unfit, there's no way they'll run a mile the first time they're going to exercise, so they'll have to figure out a series of mini-goals.

1. Continue on the flat for half a mile, repeat until happy.

2. Move along the flat for a mile, repeat until you are confident.

3. Travel uphill for half a mile, repeat to easy.

4. Move uphill a mile, repeat until you are confident.

5. Jog down on the flat for a few yards, repeat until relaxed. And so on, until they have a mile to race.

Use the acronym SMART when setting goals and set your objectives:

S = precise (something you will say for sure you can manage)

M = measurable (something you can score for success)

A = achievable (something within your ability)

R = important (something you want to achieve at this time)

T = timely (something you can achieve in a reasonable and short time).

Key skills – learning to relax fully.

It's time to start using it once you have your tape or CD, or have made your own. Arrange a time when you won't be bothered – Clarify why you need to be alone for a while if there are other people around. Remove the hook from the phone, and turn off your mobile. Lie down in a comfortable chair, or sit down and listen to the song. Don't try to judge how happy you were, just let it happen. If you fall asleep, then that's all right. If you need to be up and about at a certain time, you can also set the alarm. Do this every single day. Do this twice a day, morning and evening, if you are very nervous. If the recording helps you sleep in the night, then use it for that, but don't count it as your daytime session. Some people have trouble getting started and feel nervous about relaxing. Here are a few tips:

- Do not try to relax the first time you play it; just listen naturally and get used to the voice and words.
- If you feel very nervous and can't sit still when you're playing, make it your mission to let it run through to the end-something as long as you're playing it at least once a day.
- Don't criticize yourself if you find relaxing challenging – some people do it, some don't, it's as easy as that. When you are getting used to relaxing, be prepared for at least three weeks of playing your recording once or twice a day. This is to make it an equal chance. It is worth persevering as relaxation is such an essential part of the restoration. Keep it up throughout your recovery program once you have formed the habit of doing relaxation every day.

CHAPTER ELEVEN

EXERCISE: AN EFFECTIVE WAY OF DEALING WITH ANXIETY

Remember to consult with your doctor before beginning an exercise program. You'll need to take exercise as part of your rehabilitation routine as well as daily rest-but the good news is, you won't have to run a marathon! Exercise is helpful in many ways:

- It helps burn off stress in the muscles.
- Safe breathing helps.
- It produces beneficial chemicals in the brain.
- It allows you to reassure your body is healthy enough to deal with the effects of your anxiety. Aerobic exercise is the most effective form of exercise that is something that gets you out of breath. You would need to do it for at least 20 minutes before releasing the chemicals. That means you get the most gain from doing exercise for at least 20 minutes each time, three days a week. Many sufferers of Anxiety lose their habit of exercising, and some become severely inactive. Some forms of anxiety are very time-consuming, such as compulsive behaviors, and other types of anxiety that leave the sufferer feeling too tired to contemplate exercise.

This is a vicious cycle because the less use you make of your body, the less use you feel. And your body has been built for use – that means doing exercise that is appropriate for each person. And people with physical health issues are generally able to find a form of exercise within their ability – your doctor will be able to advise you on this. Many types of 45 exercises are done outdoors, in the fresh air, and in the natural world, and there is some evidence that this is beneficial for our mental health (but see below for housebound people's exercise tips). Place your sights to the lowest you need. If you've been in the armchair all your life, trapped in Fear, then at regular intervals, start walking around the room a little. Or if you're healthy but don't work out, get going with something easy like a park walk. It doesn't matter how long it takes you three times a week to hit the 20 minutes target-just make a start.

Exercise choices

How many anxiety patients claim they've always hated games at school are shocking. If that's you, you've got an extra degree of difficulty, but remember, there are plenty of activities you can do that is nothing like games at school. If you're a hater for exercise, then try some abstract thinking. Every physical exercise counts as long as it helps you breathe hard-scrub a floor, run up some stairs, swing your arms around. You don't need to play sports, and you don't need to enter a gym. You've just got to get active. You might also try

- Walking, particularly in the countryside or a park
- Jogging
- Line dancing
- Swimming
- Aerobics
- Social dancing
- Country dancing
- Cycling (there are special classes for the over 50s). Start with one activity once a week, and add others, so you're not getting bored.

What if you're homesick?

If your anxiety has kept you housebound, it may seem difficult to exercise, but in fact, there are plenty of choices. Tell yourself that one day you'll be able to go out and engage in other things, and exercising at home for that reason is part of your preparation. Here are some suggestions:

- Walk around the house or flat
- Walk up and down the stairs, if available
- Do housework

- Use a video or DVD workout
- Use an exercise bike or treadmill. If you're using a DVD or video workout, try finding one that isn't too hard. They always start with a warm-up session, and this is all you should try to do at first. Slowly increasing the amount of time, you can workout, and seek nothing too much for you. If you open the window when you exercise, you'll get even more value.

Establishing a personal workout routine With a standardized exercise plan, it doesn't matter how healthy or inactive you are, and you will begin to enhance your health. Look at the ladder below, and assess where you are on it. Be frank with yourself, and nobody else needs to know. Step up and downstairs Exercise video or DVD – warm-up exercise video or DVD – full exercise machine or activity of choice – once a week exercise machine or activity – twice a week exercise machine or activity – three times a week.

Using your target setting skills to figure out how to step on to the next rung of the ladder after you've got yourself on the ladder. In one hop, you can not feel ready to make a move – that's great, you can break it down into a series of small steps. Here's an example for someone who wants to move on to 20 minutes of exercise once a week, but the chosen activity doesn't match so well with that.

GOAL: join the Dance class at Beginners Ballroom.

PROBLEM: class lasts an hour; I still don't feel fit for that yet.

SOLUTION: additional repeats of video / DVD exercise before I can exercise for an hour, plus a graded sequence of walks outside the building up to one hour.

ACHIEVING LIFE BALANCE AND CONTROLLING YOUR TIME

Anxiety Disorders frequently evolve in your life after a period of stress. On the other hand, some people in their lives don't have enough tension, and their anxiety may get out of control if they have so much time to think about issues. (If that sounds like an odd idea, try to change the word 'stress' to 'challenge.' A life without any challenges is a life without motivation that contributes to boredom.) Whatever the situation, you'll need to look at the overall balance of your life to make sure it's safe, and you get what you're looking for. We all seem to ignore our own needs in times of stress and concentrate on the things we need to do. If anyone is sick and needs our support, whether there's a rush on at work, after a loss, or at some other traumatic event, our instincts take over and get us through. When the crisis is over, we breathe a sigh of relief and expect things will return to normal soon. That is the very moment when people are likely to have their first panic attack or some other Anxiety symptom. It seems so unfair to find yourself having to deal with this when you had so much on your mind, and particularly when you looked forward to a bit of peace and quiet.

Why anxiety occurs after a traumatic incident, This appears to happen for two reasons.

1. The chemicals which circulate in your body are designed to get you through during the crisis. They have adrenaline, but adrenaline is needed. It gives you the ability to handle the extra pressure that the crisis is creating. You need mental strength as well as physical energy, so if you're focused on dealing with the here and now, you're not going to have the time to brood and be concerned.

2. When the crisis is over, you're released from the need to fix the immediate problems. You will still be filled with adrenaline, which you no longer need, and your mind may start processing and responding to what has happened. Of point number 1, you can't do something. – You just need the capacity to rise to the moment; it's a very necessary human trait. Answer to item number 2. is to learn to look after yourself, to nurture yourself after the stress is over. For many people, an Anxiety disorder is a price they pay for not caring for themselves properly. It's as if a small voice inside you has been asking for your attention, and when you ignore that voice, it eventually decides to yell and shout by hitting you with a panic attack, phobia, or compulsion.

Despite this, many people feel guilty about taking care of themselves. They put their work, their family, their chores at home ahead of their own needs. Are you one of them? There is no need to feel guilty about looking after yourself – if you do this, you will be more able to look after others. The same is true if your life is without challenges. If you don't have money worries or physical health worries, and if everything you want is right there for you, you could well feel guilty about acknowledging that you still aren't happy. After all, so many other people have it much tougher than you. But knowing that doesn't make you feel any better, does it? And it doesn't make your anxiety go away. Just like someone who has too much stress, you need to make changes so that you can get better. Feeling guilty is just a waste of energy.

ASSESSING YOUR LIFE BALANCE

Use your journal to keep track of how you spend a whole week of your time. Shortly, you can see if you quit for your own needs at any time. Here's an example of a day from a working parent's notebook: 07.30 get up, shower, breakfast, make packed lunches, drop kids at school 09.15 late to work again, better skip lunch 17.30 leave work, pick up shopping, take the oldest child to activity 19.00 eat with partner and children, my turn to wash up 20.00 my turn to put kids to bed, usual arguments 21.00 check emails, telephone childminder, Of course, some days are just very busy, but if the entire diary were like this, then that person would have to think things through and make changes. How painful it would be if they dealt with an anxiety disorder as well, and yet that is just what other people have to do. In the above example, even on this busy day, the following adjustments might be possible: * Teach the kids how to make their own lunch, under supervision, allowing more time for the school and work trip. Then it won't be appropriate to miss lunch, and in the busy day, the lunch break may turn into a small window of rest.

- Find out why bedtime is triggering disputes, and seek to make it more fun.
- Demand that someone else takes over the fixture list. You may still feel like you don't really have time for yourself, but you

need to take some time for yourself as part of your recovery from anxiety. As easy as a soothing bath, watching your favorite TV show, or reading a magazine, it can be anything. This is just as critical as all other rehabilitation aspects, so don't skimp on it.

IMPLEMENTING LIFESTYLE CHANGES

By now, you've come to know that recovery from anxiety requires a lot of time. Yet no need to be dismayed. Remember to start small and continue to be careful with each process – it will take time for the changes to have an impact. Summary of tasks so far:

- Keep an anxiety diary
- Score your anxiety
- Set goals
- Do the simple exercise of breathing.

By now, you will have the following in place:

- Relaxation every day
- Daily exercise, aiming for three days a week building up to 20 minutes
- Changes in your were required
- Improvements in the intake of caffeine if required
- Improvements in alcohol, nicotine and other substance use if needed
- A program for better sleep if needed
- A program to allow more time for yourself if needed

If you haven't managed all of these, don't worry, because it takes time. The important thing is that you now understand what you need to do, and you have learned not to be intimidated by the task's size because you know that it is best to take small steps. Dealing with demanding tasks You can find some of those tasks especially difficult. Take it more slowly if that is the case, and be prepared to work harder. It's possible that the job you consider most challenging is the one you need to do the most and the one that will offer you the most benefit if you succeed. Often, one or more of the tasks can be challenging as they contribute to your specific anxiety. For example

Relaxation

You may be scared to let go. Exercise: You can be afraid to faint, or hurt your heart. Food: You may be afraid to be sick or surprised, or you may be concerned with food hygiene.

Sleep

You may be afraid to let go again, or you may be afraid to get more involved. More challenges: You may be afraid to take too much on. If you have this extra level of difficulty, then you will need to use the anxiety-challenging skills that we will discuss in the chapters below to help you to complete your lifestyle changes. The distinction between a reluctance to make adjustments and an anxiety-driven challenge is crucial to consider. For example, if you feel you can't make time for a therapy plan because your OCD is too time-consuming, then making time is your struggle – just five minutes a day would help. However, if your OCD is primarily based on one of the things, you'll need to concentrate on it as part of your key treatment plan instead of modifying your lifestyle.

CHAPTER TWELVE

HANDLING STRESSFUL SITUATIONS

It seems as normal to many people who encounter stress as eating or sleeping. Indeed, overeating, sleepless nights, and aches and pains frequently result directly from stress. Although some stress is innate — think about every human being's fight-or-flight response — a lot of the stress you feel zaps your strength and makes you less efficient. If you were feeling acceptable levels of tension, you'd still have resources for other things. Unfortunately, you could be burning through your resources as a result of excessive tension, feeling as exhausted as a dishrag most of the time. You can't cope when tough circumstances occur, because you're tired and drained. The stress-related issue of self-talk is a bit like the chicken and the egg.

What happens first?

Does your negative self-talk increase your anxiety and the resulting stress levels, or does the existence of stress lead to negative self-talk and self-flagellation in your life? Although pondering can be fascinating, solving this question isn't important — we know they both feed on each other. What's crucial is finding out what causes tension. That's where negative self-talk starts in and leads you down a negative path leading to rising stress. You know by now that this situation is hurting your negative self-talk. It clouds your view and restricts your choices. You should know that you can see when negative self-talk begins when you recognize your causes, stop it in its tracks, turn it into positive self-talk, and give yourself more choices to relieve stress.

Watching It Happen.

Think about a situation that is causing you anxiety. You know that feeling — you start getting nervous. It could make your palms sweaty. Your breathing is getting shallow and fast. You could get a nervous tic, or you maybe bite your fingernails. You could be speaking too fast or being unable to speak coherently. You might start imagining horrible things happening. Your heartbeat is getting faster, and your throat is tightening even though nothing seems wrong. You can never say, "I'm tired" to yourself. You may not know how tension grows over time and takes away more and more of your energy. At some point, you just realize you're feeling awful. The headaches are taking a toll; you are swallowing so many stomach acid pills, and no matter what you do, you can't fall asleep at night.

Say: "Hi! "Sad self-talk enjoys attention to The Sad Self-talk. It likes to feed on and use stressful circumstances to tell you why your life is a mess. It is a strange phenomenon. You may think that your negative self-talk gives you ideas to get out of the tension, that helping you evaluate what is going on is a companion. But in fact, the negative self-talk feeds on your stressed state, and the negative self-talk increases your stressed state. You are losing the ability to handle life effectively. It is important to notice where negative self-talk kicks in during stressful times, so you can catch it and turn your attention to more positive self-talk. Let's look at a variety of stress-related circumstances that people struggle with.

Acting out Stress

Stress manifests in a physical form in many panic attacks. On your chest, you feel a crushing weight as if you have a heart attack. You can breathe or suck in an exaggerated fashion. You may develop tics, breathe in an exaggerated way, tap your fingers. You may develop tics, quickly tap your fingers, or constantly cross your legs, and uncross them. They have one thing in common — your body gets involved with all of these interactions you can relate to. In addition to the tension that is driving you, you have a physical reaction or feeling. For example, if you could step outside of your body, you might see the nervous tic. You could see yourself squeezing your chest while trying to relieve the crushing weight you're feeling. The good news is, you should start looking at your patterns. You should start diagnosing how you and your body are responding to stressful conditions.

Think of the responses which are overwhelming. Physically, what happens to you when you get so depressed or so upset that you can't function? Write them down. You might write, for example, "I get intermittent panic attacks when I drive on the highway late at night. I continue to hyperventilate and sweat. I have to open the window to let the air in because I get overheated and have a hard time focusing on driving. If you're not sure how you're responding, bring your smartphone or some other computer with a small notebook or form notes. Notice what happens when you perceive a physical reaction that is coming on. How would you react? What are your feelings?

What physical reaction happens?

Note these as they occur, and follow trends. Don't analyze the "why"; just watch what's going on so you can get more comfortable with your own pattern.

Recognizing the signs

Once you're completely in the grasp of the oppressive situation, it's hard to "step outside" yourself and pull back. Recognizing the onset of physical symptoms would also be operated upon. You want to know when the pressure starts mounting. You want to realize that your stress levels are escalating so you can make different choices — but to realize it, you have to recognize how different choices are manifested — but to realize it, you have to recognize how it manifests within you.

No one-size-fits-all solution.

You need to be able to determine or diagnose how circumstances impact you. And when you can see what's happening, do you want to make new decisions and put in constructive self-talk to help. When the physical responses have been identified, back up to what causes them. In this book, you've learned a lot about triggers, and you should keep challenging the triggers that start dragging you down the proverbial rabbit hole and into more negative self-talk. Think of the circumstances which are stressing you. What happens just before the physical reactions start to happen? Will you think anything? Do you feel anything? Anything goes wrong? Or are they simply random? You still can't tell what begins the loop and causes your negative reactions to come to you?

Here, there are no correct or incorrect responses. This is what you are feeling. Note all in your report that you are conscious of.

Holding Your Negative Reactions Accountable

Next, think of these negative reactions as "visitors." The physical reactions that you have are temporary residents of your body, but they are not really yours. The circumstances can be real, but there are no stressful automated responses. Those are habits learned. They are responses that you've learned, and you've started wearing them as your own, but you can choose to uninvite them and make a different choice at any moment. Positive self-talk can be of benefit to you. As for tension, here are some of the constructive self-talk choices that you have at your fingertips. If you think you are entering a stressful situation or if your body tells you that a negative visitor has taken up residence there, you may want to call on these.

Phase One

Study this list and circle those encouraging words of self-talk that have meaning to you. Which ones induce peace for you while you read will line? What ones resonate with you, and seem to calm you down? What ones can you only refer to? "It is to come, too. This is a time point; it's not the whole of my life." "I'm bigger than any situation I face. I've been forced to deal with my life and everything that comes to me. '"I'm cool. I feel comfortable. I monitor my own reactions." "I can't help feeling uptight. It throws me down. So I'm making different decisions." "I have the option of taking a deep breath. Breathe in slowly and breathe out slowly. Each breath out eliminates the poison from my body, and every breath in it replaces it with soothing, healing warmth." "I lose my toughness every time I give in to fear and stress. I'm in charge and holding my focus." "I'm going into my personal zone. I am tough. I'm in control of my life and my reactions." "I don't belong to the negative emotions that visit me. I am not welcoming them. I just welcome constructive, safe reactions. I have a clean body; my mind is calm, and I feel fine.

Phase Two

As you review this list of options for positive self-talk, circle those that resonate with you. If none of them seem to suit, write down a version that sounds more appropriate to you. You're going to want to practice these until they become mantras for you. In certain instances within this book, you have looked at some different scenarios for which you will be able to prepare or schedule ahead of time. For panic attacks, widespread anxiety disorder, OCD, or advancement. You may not know when the stress will come on you in the case of panic attacks, generalized anxiety disorder, OCD, or the like. On a beautiful sunny day, you could be walking down the street, and all of a sudden, the panic attack jumps from behind you. Because of that, the development of a mantra is important. Having some positive self-talk at the ready is important, waiting for you to call on it. Structure your day in a way to practice these mantras during the day so that you are in a position to call them at any time. Because you'll have to close your eyes, read through these instructions a few times, so you know what to do. Start this exercise when you're ready. That one needs ongoing involvement. Because you don't know when you're going to need it, each day you have to practice the "waiting" and preparing.

Step Three

Find a quiet spot each day to sit down for a few minutes. Do so at least three to four times every day for three to five minutes at a time. Take a deep breath in three times, and picture warm, clean air filling the lungs and body. Imagine all stress, all negativity, and all concern leaving your body when you exhale. Breathe this way until you feel your body becoming calmer and more tranquil. Just close your eyes when you're ready, and your breathing is deep and calming. Only sit down and concentrate on your breath for a few minutes. Imagine that as you exhale, you can see the air filling your lungs and how it exists. Focus only on the breath; gently brush aside thoughts or words that come into your mind. Imagine the inside of your head is a guy with a broom. Kindly he brushes away any feelings he wants to visit. If you have a phobia towards brooms — or men — imagine another picture that works for you like this.

Repeat your mantra to yourself over and over while you sit quietly. You might say it quietly as a whisper under your breath, or you might just say it in your head without speaking out loud at all. Imagine the words when you think without thinking out loud at all as best you can. Only imagine the words as you speak them as best you can. Some people prefer applying a musical ring to the words and others like chanting them. Some are fond of incorporating modulation or a somber tone. Whatever helps you catch these words, makes them last, and it's right for you to give them affect. With this mantra, make sure you spend the entire three to five minutes. Feel calm in your body. Know how the deep breathing calms you down. Don't panic into this. And with all you've got to do, nine to twelve minutes out of your day won't get you farther behind. Instead, once you're through the workout, you can find that you're happier and more energized to finish what you need to do.

This exercise is extremely important to do every single day. When they come to visit, you want to be ready for the stressors. You need to have a plan for taking another course of action.

Practice Makes perfect

You may want to write meaningful self-talk on a card you are bringing with you. Or you may want to put a few notes around to remind you of your mantra. The more you use it, the faster it is when you need to call on it. The next important step is to take it into the picture when the physical stress reaction begins to visit you.

Make yourself aware of the situations which stress you.

If you know that while driving at night, you tend to have a panic attack, then practice your positive self-talk for a few minutes before you go out. If you have OCD and know that you are prone to constantly checking your home to make sure that all is as it should be, practice the sayings every time you are about to leave. To make constructive self-talk work for you, you have to evaluate and plan when you need it.

Preparing for Stressful Life Conditions

We described a generalized stress reaction earlier. It can happen anywhere without much warning at any given time. Of course, you'll know that occasionally something potentially negative will happen. You are also hoping for the best but expect the worst. In these cases, your negative self-talk helps ratchet up your anxiety. The outcome can actually be positive or negative, but your negative self-talk will always assure you that the worst is waiting around the corner for you. The truth is life is in difficult situations. There are suffering and sorrow. People who we love die. People are getting sick and crying. People are losing work and families. Good self-talk doesn't make you delude into believing real isn't real. You're not going to believe that everything is perfect because it isn't. What constructive self-talk will do is provide you with a better outlook to get through those tough or negative times.

- It's helping you get through these tough or tragic times in a different way.
- It will help you concentrate your attention, explain your ideas, and give you the strength to complete whatever tasks are ahead of you.
- Think of someone who you know has been terminally ill but has kept a good attitude. That person did not believe he would be "saved" by the positive mindset, but he wanted to enjoy the time he had. Think of people who have been through a divorce but have decided to remain friends, even for their children's sake.
- Think of someone who might have been fired from a job, unable to pay her bills, but yet worked in a shelter for the homeless. There are people who are struggling in life through very tough and traumatic circumstances and seemingly come out well. One guy who I knew was put in jail for

something that he didn't do. He kept a positive outlook, declined to consider those years as wasted, and then turned the experience into something that others benefited from. If negative self-talk is "right," why is it that not everybody is cracking under the weight of difficulty? Since your preferred self-talk always determines your desire to be optimistic, find solutions, and focus on the silver lining.

Stop the Panic!

Most people who are going through a difficult time simply want to have it over. "I can't wait until my divorce is finished." "I wish they'd just give me the pink slip, and get it done. The waiting is killing me." "When this year comes to an end, I'll be so relieved! "Instead of plowing through these negative situations, let's look at ways you can use them to practice your positive self-discussion and possibly adopt a new attitude or approach to dealing with what you are going through. Think of an upcoming event that causes stress to you or one that you are going through now. Write down what could happen and what you predict.

So, you could write, for example: "My company is in financial trouble. Layoffs happened all over me. I felt the trouble, though. Layoffs happened all over me. Via the grapevine, I heard my unit is next. It's just a matter of time before I get my pink slip. "Now — this is important — write out from this situation on what you expect to happen to you. People also tell themselves a story about how the event is going to kill them. You could write, for example: "If I lose my job I can't send my children to college. I can't even pay household mortgages. Outside there are no jobs. I'm destined to eat cat food alive — and what do I feed my cats? We are all going to starve to death. "Make sure to take the time to write this down. Most of what you're going to write about this situation is simply the negative self-talk that comes to visit you. These are the views that you now hold on how your life will be impacted by this coming situation. You can write these findings and feel sure that they're going to happen, but you're actually writing a play at this moment. It's true that your business may be facing layoffs, and you may be next, but what comes after that is just the imagination fuelled by your negative self-talk.

Next, pinpoint your tools. Identify certain qualities, abilities, support structures, analytical skills, and strengths that you possess that could help you cope more effectively with the situation ahead. You could write, for example: "I am a very good employee. I give my employer a lot of interest because nobody else knows how to run the program that I do. "Or," I've been through difficult times before. I still manage to pick myself up, dust off myself, and start again! "The next section of this exercise is critically important as it will ask you to challenge the values that you are possibly very close to you. You can genuinely believe, for example, that the self-talk you are using on the upcoming event is real. They're going to eat cat food. You are never going to get any other job. You're doomed to death. What you need to do next is shed a strong light on those convictions, and look closely at them. At this level, they're beliefs only. They are not true evidence.

The reality is that there are several potential consequences of any case. Some results you may prefer more than others, but there are many ways in which your life could turn you into more than others, but there are many ways that your life may turn out. You don't really know what's coming around the corner before the final act. There is both a positive and a negative aspect in most situations. Yeah, it's hard if your life's love leaves you for another guy, but it's also freeing that you don't live with someone who lied to you anymore. Yeah, going to prison for a crime you haven't committed is a horrific tragedy, but taking those experiences, writing about them, and trying to reform a broken system is a positive outcome. Many causes and movements are initiated when someone encounters something so awful that they don't want someone else to have to go through it. In other words, transforming a negative result into a positive one is almost always possible.

Now you might say, "She's got rose-colored glasses on. She's trying to paint a perfect image in which one doesn't belong. "That's why loosening the long-held convictions just a little is important. If you are not going to consider that there may be another way of looking at a difficult situation, then there is no point in completing this exercise. If you want more control, more opportunities, and more energy to cope with stress, you need to let go of the illusion that you "know" what's right and wrong, and that you "know" what's going to happen next.

Write down two explanations concerning the present situation. Create a story with two potential positive outcomes in them. This can require some imaginative writing on your part, but force yourself to think of two ways in which the situation could go and might have some positive attributes.

Let's go back, for example, to the situation at work where you are expecting the pink slip. Two possible outcomes could include: "I did such a good job here, and I am highly valued. They can't lay off anyone, so I will be here for a long time to come even though it hurts me to see my friends in pain and lose their jobs. I'll take a good outlook and remain calm throughout the process. "Or you might think alternatively:" I might lose my work, but the truth is I loved it here. Something else I would want to do, but I was too afraid to go. It's something different when I get the pink slip, but I was too afraid to resign. If I get the pink slip, I'll be inspired to pursue my dreams. It may be financially difficult, but I'll find a way to make it work. If I look hard enough, there's always a solution. "The point of creating these two options is to show you that there isn't just one foregone conclusion about how the stressful life situation ends. You tell yourself a story by negative self-talk — you write the plotline, and "think" how it all works out. And the stress level keeps increasing.

There is no other way, apparently. You can see that there are other potential outcomes by pushing yourself to write on other choices. During times of difficulty, if your self-talk is based exclusively on how awful it all is, you can not give yourself the ability to recharge your batteries or see any positive results. You should use constructive self-talk in the midst of coping with something to calm yourself down and find opportunities to concentrate on something other than the anxiety or frustration that the situation has brought on. There are situations even when a close friend or relative dies of a terminal illness in which people can find joy in small ways — maybe by caring for the individual. Even when you're with someone who's dying, old wounds get healed, or things that haven't been spoken before are spoken.

You will also sometimes let go of past hurts or difficulties.

It's not to say that actually looking on the bright side is the answer to stress — it isn't. You have to be realistic and objective about whatever challenges you face. And I'm not saying that you're not going to have to deal with difficult emotions as you go through the challenging life experiences. But being exhausted and under stress weakens the power. You need to be forceful and clear-headed. You always have the chance to use your self-talk to direct the situation and your reaction to it. Your self-talk can either defeat you early on or give you the ability to remain open and curious about what my next happen.

Managing Life on Overload

The introduction of technology was intended to make life simpler for everyone. Quick access to information, the ability to complete "on-the-fly" tasks, and increased communication were meant to free up time and allow people to focus on what matters to them. Unfortunately, it's done the exact opposite for most of them. Growing technology keeps many people linked 24/7, enabling the transom to absorb an overwhelming flood of information. The need to review messages in several occupations permeates family dinners, holidays, and leisure time in the evenings. It is not relaxing for most people to be able to be online at all hours of the day or night searching for details and gain access to new details to process; instead, it raises the level of tension or concern.

People still struggle with time management. How can I get it all done in a given day? Children have places they need to be; there are errands to run and projects to complete, and the job begins to pile up more and more on top of all this. The stress rates the average person is coping with tend to increase every day.

Too stressed? You're Playing!

In a 2010 study, the American Psychological Association found that "Americans typically understand that their stress levels remain elevated and surpass what they find acceptable. Adults tend to recognize the value of healthy habits, such as controlling their stress rates, eating well, having enough sleep and exercise, but also experiencing difficulties in implementing these healthy behaviors. They mention being too busy as a primary obstacle that prevents them from handling their stress better, and lack of motivation, resources, and time as the key reasons why they are not more physically active. In this study again, lack of commitment was cited as a deterrent to making healthier habits when a health care provider suggested improvements in lifestyle. But most assume that resilience can be gained and strengthened if they only have more time and motivation. "Everyday Stress Creates One of the daily stress issues is that it is subtle. You may not "look" overwhelmed, but you unexpectedly lift your voice in frustration or start feeling discouraged and depressed. You note you grit your teeth or cut your nails. Every day, stress creeps in, and your negative self-talk fuels the stressful fires unknown to you. You get cut off by a car on the highway, and you wonder, What's wrong with people?

The planet is becoming such a gross and fearsome place. Somebody with fifteen items gets in front of you in the checkout line for ten items or less. Look? You tell yourself. People everywhere are rude. This planet is going to really go potting. At home, where you want to enjoy your abode sanctuary, your child is calling you a name that is not fit to repeat here. Your self-talk is continually dwelling on these circumstances, and you are mulling about how awful everything has been and how horrible your life is. That's how stress — and its criminal partner, negative self-talk — steals from you. They join forces and zap your strength, cloud your view, and give you a negative and self-defeating insight into the universe. You can understand it all, of course: there was a very rude person on the freeway; somebody cut you in line, and you were very disrespectful to your kid. The problem is, you then made the option of allowing negative self-talk to take over and stack the trouble until you were unable to work positively.

Uncovering Secrets

Like many of the things you'll discover in this book, there's stealthy daily tension. It comes in cases where you don't want to. No one wants to be cut off on the highway and put in danger, but instead of allowing the situation to be what it is, the mind is likely to take control of it and make it a huge negative case. Staying aware and alert to those issues that cause your negative self-talk is of the utmost importance with daily stress. That needs dedication and resources. You should stop because the disappointment is actually easier to give in. Yet you can change that, with the power of the mind. This is an option to switch from the negative self-talk to constructive self-talk. And if you can't control the things that happen to you, you can control your reaction to them.

Move Out of the Tornado

Some walk into an unscathed storm, and some are swept away by the winds. You can stand amid a raging emotional storm but refuse to take part in it. How? How? Through becoming more conscious of the events you experience in your day that cause anxiety within you, and then noticing the negative reactions that build upon yourself. It needs the patience to get out of the tornado. It needs you to be aware of the things that happen to you all day long. It would be beneficial to always bring a small notebook with you for this exercise or to use the note app on your smartphone or tablet. You want to keep a running list of items that happen to you so you can take some time to analyze them.

Think of a moment in an ordinary situation where you've been going through something unpleasant. For example, for your son's graduation, maybe you wanted to be back home, so you were due to catch a plane. You've been stuck in awful traffic due to a highway crash. You heard the tick of the clock, ticked, ticked, and in your car, you sat still and knew the plane would leave without you. Perhaps the plane left without you, and in the terminal, you screamed or cried, realizing that you would miss the proud face of your son as they gave him the diploma. That certainly was a collection of distressing and stressful incidents. But remember what happened next. Another flight left to your destination, and you ended up joining your friend. You saw photos of the graduation and were sad that you couldn't be there, but you did something with your son to celebrate and thereby appreciate his success. The anxious moment in the car that watched the clock tick slowly faded out of your mind. In the past, you're thinking about it like in,

"Remember the time. ."The purpose of stepping outside the tornado is to evoke the post-moment while you are still in the moment. You know, "This too will pass," even in the thick of trouble. To do so, you have to call for constructive self-talk.

Decide to keep a diary.

Take notes of stressful situations throughout the day for two weeks; this will help you see patterns, triggers and get a glimpse of things that seem stressful at the time, but then lose their power over you. Decide to capture everything you can while you embark on this process. Only because you're writing a report, don't forget stuff that seems unimportant! For instance, you might be inclined to reduce a case because writing it down seems stupid. Be honest with yourself. There are no rights or wrongs — stress comes to us from several different directions. Capture everything that your mind is having a reaction to or that you view as negative.

If you skip a day, keep recording happenings until you have two weeks of data that you can work with. Be sure not only to catch the occurrence but also your negative reaction to it. Jot down a few words about the frustration that you felt next to the event: "helpless," "overwhelmed," "angry." Study the stressors. If the material has been collected, take a look at what you have learned. There are patterns to it? Do some stressors appear to occur more often than others? Is it a number of stressors, some major and some small, or do you notice that a lot of minor irritations occur every day? Or, conversely, are the seemingly large things just stressing you? Look closely at the descriptors you've written alongside the events. What trends do you see in this? Do you react the most often with anger? Do you feel really disillusioned? Do you feel powerless in coping with stressors in your life, and without resources?

It's critically important that you have some understanding of the stressors and about your responses before you can make constructive self-talk work for you. Don't miss these steps — take the time to go through some detail about your own situation. When you are more conscious of what is upsetting you and how you are responding, you will begin to incorporate constructive self-talk into your day. Start the morning with the use of constructive self-talk to frame your experiences to come. For this initial exercise, using a mirror to talk to yourself. Talk to yourself explicitly, and emphasize the claims.

"It's a regular day. There are going to be unpleasant things happening to me. That is life. I have choices about how to respond. Today, I want to maintain my personal control." "I can move outside the storm anytime I want. I don't need to get my own negative self-talk pulled along. I will release it as soon as I know it. It's my decision. '"Things are going to happen. I'm responding. Today I choose how to respond, and I choose constructive self-talk." "I welcome tough circumstances, as they teach me something almost always. They let me improve my attitude and practice my positive self-talk." "Life is about learning. I watch other people. I look at the circumstances. I've learned something from all that happens to me." "The most important thing for me is to hang on to my personal strength. Throughout the day, I remain focused on my optimistic approach. "It's important that your self-talk statements aren't fake to you. There will be stuff that will cause you during the day. There will probably be things that will cause you the day there will be stuff. Possibly there would be things you don't like and choose not to deal with. There are occasions when you slip into old habits. You use these ideas to set your mind in a different direction, to react differently, and to adapt to what is going to happen to you.

Now, build some constructive self-talk solutions you can invoke when stressors arise during the day. You may want to write these cards on 3 "or 5" cards or place them on notepaper that you can hold. Some people post these in their cars, computers, or wallets. Keep them handy so that you can contact them when you need to. Review the list and decide which of these fits your style and circumstance, or use this same method to compose a couple of your own.

"I can live with whatever life throws at me. I'm calm; I'm confident, and I'm making my own decisions." "Situations happen, but with negative self-talk, I don't need to intensify them. I have taken a different direction." "Look what's going on right now. It's a storm, but I decide to move outside. The view is better looking in from the outside." "Tomorrow (or next month, next year, etc.), this situation will probably not matter to me either. I won't devote my attention to it today." "Things are happening. People are human beings. With negative self-talk, I don't need to make this situation worse. "So, critically, when the unpleasant or negative occurrence happens, instead of giving in to negative self-talk, turn your focus to something that is better for you. Some people bring a song they want to sing along with them. Some people bring photographs of children or animals that will calm them down. Some people go for a stroll, look out the window or jumping jacks! Have something ready to do if the awkward situation happens.

How is it working in the real world?

Imagine the situation with the car being cut off from you on the highway. Your immediate response is to see to it that you are free. Then, the self-talk you have selected kicks in: "Things happen. People are human beings. I am free. Then, the self-talk you have selected kicks in: "Things happen. People are human beings. With negative self-talk, I don't have to make this situation worse. "You're beginning to hum your soothing album ... Or you start reminding your kids of a fun holiday. Maybe you're repeating your favorite verse from a poem. Your focus moves from the present situation to something that calms you down and makes you feel more relaxed. The "rude" person has crossed your vision line by now and is driving down the highway to cut off the next driver — and probably having a ticket. On the other hand, you drive with a more relaxed disposition and temperament.

CREATING TIME AND SPACE TO RECHARGE:

Taking care of yourself.

One way that stress does damage is that many people stop taking care of themselves in response to it. They are not running or eating right. They're losing sleep. They are too nervous or too busy to go searching for friends or companions. As compared to a deliberate preparation mode, they are in response mode. Even when people really need to take care of themselves, they're least focused on it. Here's another place to turn to constructive self-talk that will help you calm down and channel your energies. The loop goes like this: over things, you feel anxious. You just don't care about yourself. You are thinking to yourself about how bad you are, and you don't know about yourself. "I know I should go to the gym to alleviate my tension, but I'm too wigged out to do so." You know the decisions you're making aren't the best ones for you, but negative self-talk comes in again and tells you that you have to act the way you're doing, that you can't do anything different, and that this is all there is. For instance, if you know that you "will" take better care of yourself but your self-talk doesn't let you, it's time to make a different choice.

Next, ask yourself if there is anything you should do better, something that could help you deal with the stressors in your life more effectively. Need some more sleep? Want to make healthier food choices? Want to get more workout? Set a goal of what you want to do. Refer to Chapter 7 for ways to use constructive self-talk in making a life change if you want to control your stress by seeking a new career or making more money. In this section, we'll discuss the need to take better care of yourself to be stronger in coping with the general stressors in your life.

Determine what else you need to do.

Write what you should do for yourself in your journal that could give you more motivation or be happier while you handle stress. Now write down why you don't do that now. Who is it that holds you back? What are the obstacles? Be frank here, and gather all the excuses you can not make the choices you need to make. Be careful that in this chapter, you are not concentrating on big life decisions; these are discussed elsewhere in this book and require a separate set of exercises. You might say, for example, that you need to work out more often and get more exercise, but maybe you are working three jobs. If that is the case, you need a shift in overall life. Nonetheless, you might write in this section that you just can not adhere to an exercise schedule.

You know you need one, but there's never anything you enjoy doing over and over again. Identify the negative self-talk associated with why you are unable to take the steps that you know you need to take. It may be issues such as "I hate exercise" or "I can't afford to eat nutritious food so I buy garbage" or "I'm only at that stage of life where I can't sleep very well. It happens to everybody. "Write down the words that you use and the stuff that comes to mind if you talk to someone else and try to persuade her why you can't do what you know to anyone else and try to convince her why you can't do what you think you can.

You'll be using the constructive self-talk in this next segment to improve behavior. First, set a reasonable, creditable, and practical goal for yourself. For example, you might set a goal: I'll go to bed fifteen minutes earlier each night for the next five nights until I'm going to bed more than an hour earlier than I was. "Or you might write," I'm going to pick carrots at the store when I shop this week instead of chips. "Or," I'm going to take a walk with my spouse every night for thirty minutes after dinner. Here you are trying to make a life change, and you want to take it one step at a time. If you have not worked out at all, it's probably unrealistic to set a goal of working out for an hour six days a week. Focus on what is fair, reliable, and realistic.

Now, establish constructive phrases of self-talk to support you with your efforts.

Depending on the target you have selected, those will be different. If you've worked in this book through other parts, you'll have some ideas about how to improve those. Examples for some common scenarios are given here. You may use one of these, or compose a couple of your own. "In my life, I wish to make this change. It will help me to control my depression with greater ease." "Every day is a new day. Today I'm determined to make the right decisions for me." "My target is sensible. Every day, I will take action to ensure that my goal is my life." "I need all the strength and support I can get. I make the choices that give me greater access to my personal resources." "Why do I want to do things in the world that are not good for me? I know what's right, and I choose for myself. "Once you've set your target, and learned the positive self-talk that works for you, spend at least fifteen minutes each day talking to you, spend at least fifteen minutes each day sitting quietly and imagining a less stressed person. Image yourself or imagine making the choices that are right for you. Imagine that you get the sleep you need, eat the food you need, or take walks every night. Using all your feelings and creativity to feel confident about what you've done. Experience the good feelings that come from being more relaxed and more at ease, ready to deal with everything that comes along the way.

Repeat 'I am optimistic self-talk' again and again, while you sit and imagine. Keep your mind on what you want and not what you don't want. Know, to successfully handle the stress and you need to have the resources to do so.

Take care of your time and your life - In today's world, there are few people who wouldn't agree they need more hours in the day. You never seem to have enough time to do anything you want or need to do. Some people work two or three jobs, jumping from one job to the next.

Parents with kids seem to have countless commitments: sports and attendance schedules, school activities, dates to play. In reality, in today's culture, most people are constantly finding so many places to go and things to do. Life rolls back and forth.

Anxiety grows with the to-dos list rising longer and longer.

Time is difficult to handle as it gives you a set 24 hours a day, seven days a week. How can you handle anything that's not versatile or malleable? You must then learn to control yourself. Controlling time is about controlling yourself.

CHAPTER THIRTEEN

EFFECTIVE TIPS ON HOW TO DEAL WITH ANXIETY AND PROCRASTINATION

In this chapter, we will look at how to avoid procrastination and ensuring that you do not develop that late minute rush and anxiety over your tasks. Sometimes, we feel there is a lot of time on our hands to do our jobs. However, we end up procrastinating and not doing our best the deliver on the said task. I will be explaining detailed steps on how to better handle our time, deal with distractions, and ultimately reduce stress and anxiety in our daily lives. Here goes:

Stage 1: Start the task.

Get moving, regardless of whether you have failed previously. If you plan to win, you should start. This appears glaringly evident; however, if you have been procrastinating on something, that is the best time to start it. This step will show that it has taken the first grand step to become very successful in life

Stage 2: Set out a deadline to get the job done

We will talk about this point in more detail in a later area in this part. The odds are remote that you will ever complete anything without it getting booked into your schedule. We always wait because we don't close off the first time to complete the activity.

Stage 3: Break the activity into small parts

You will never begin shedding pounds if you see the entire project in one gym session. A heavy drinker would experience issues envisioning himself not drinking for the remainder of his/her life. Anybody can deal with not drinking for 24 hours.

"one day, one step at a time" is a famous slogan among self-help groups. It is the acknowledgment of a critical truth of our experience: We live our whole lives in the here and now. What else will we do with it?.

Stage 4. Embrace a 'Do it now' mindset.

Individuals who overcome procrastination issues figure out how to progress toward becoming 'Do It Now'ers.' They never hold up until tomorrow to do what they know ought to be done today. They set things back after each use. They won't delay.

Stage 5. Set destinations.

We all know the important requirements for setting goals for our everyday life, but we must repeat it here because it affects our ability to stop procrastinating. Set a goal to accomplish something you have procrastinated about doing today.

Stage 6. Audit your achievements.

Successful people in life harp on their small wins. Losers always center around their disappointments. It is of incentive to help yourself to remember zones where you have prevailing with regards to winning the hesitation game.

Stage 7. Reward or rebuff yourself.

I am not supporting immoral conduct by proposing you overcome procrastinating issues by rebuffing yourself. What I am recommending is that you discover an effective method for punishing yourself for the practices that aid procrastination in your life. For example, not accomplishing things you said you would do in record time. One supervisor I know purchases his staff lunch out of his pocket if he doesn't have his reports on a schedule. On the off chance that he vows to convey something and hesitates, at that point, he needs to fork out money, and for him, this is negative support for negative conduct.

Also, if you have prevailed with regards to carrying out a responsibility you have since quite a while ago procrastinated about doing, compensate yourself. We will, in general, recurrent those practices for which we get encouraging feedback and disregard those practices, which result in negative fortification.

TAKING CARE OF DISTRACTIONS

If interruptions become an issue for you, utilize the five stages recorded below. To figure out what is an issue with disruption, ask yourself, "Am I accepting small interruptions during high-priority moments of my life?" In this way, practice these means to check the time wasted while attending to such interruptions.

Schedule the free days on your calendar

A lot of individuals think the only time you are genuinely 'occupied' is the point at which you have somebody with you. A secretary checked her Supervisor's office, sees nobody, and erroneously assumes he/she is less busy. There is nothing wrong with scheduling time in your everyday organizer that will enable you to maintain a strategic distance from the time-squandering movement called interferences.

Inform the people around you that you can't be interrupted

If you need to take out interruptions, ensure you have a 'no interference' periods in your daily schedule. Tell others you can't be disturbed in any way, shape, or form unless the office building is on fire! And only if the fire is moving toward the floor underneath you! Achieving your goals requires desperate measures, and this is just one of them.

Whenever you are interrupted, stand up.

Do you need a strategy guaranteed to reduce interruption time to the barest minimal? Stand up when an interrupter comes into the room and stay standing while they talk. They will before long get the message, 'Be quick I'm occupied.'

Let us analyze this example, "If somebody comes into your space to interrupt you and you welcome them in, and you sit in a relaxed position, put your feet up on the work area, and offer them a cup of coffee." What message would you say you are passing on to them? Of course, the message would look like this - "enter, take a seat, make yourself comfortable, and let's talk. What I was doing isn't so important; waste my time in any capacity you deem fit!"

Make fewer trips through the office.

This may appear to be somewhat simple, yet would you say you are mindful what amount of time is squandered in a day by running for an espresso, water, and the washroom? Become mindful that when you leave your work region. Your goals are more important than some side attractions.

60 PRACTICALTIMEMANAGEMENT TIPS TO HELP YOU REDUCE ANXIETY

1. When wiping out wardrobes, storerooms, and so forth., mark three containers: "scrap, give away, and keep."
2. If you haven't utilized something in over a year, don't give it a chance to occupy the prime room.
3. Schedule a 'tranquil hour' every day and think of it as non-debatable.
4. Try not to give others a chance to infringe on your significant "personal-time."
5. Each night, set out all that you will require in the first part of the day.
6. Utilize your arranging schedule to plan your schedules.
7. Calendar "arrangements" with yourself.
8. Have an office in your home for composing and recording.
9. Exploit self-inking stamps to spare time.
10. Agent at whatever point conceivable.
11. Complete things during the specified time.
12. Make meals in two-folds and freeze them to save you some cooking time.
13. Toss out however much correspondence and other administrative work as could reasonably be expected.
14. Store adornments in egg containers inside a cabinet.

15. Keep an inventory of every item used regularly, for example, paper products, lights, trash packs, paper cuts, Post-it Notes.

16. Settle on minor choices rapidly.

17. Try not to sit around anguishing after choices.

18. Store things near where they will be utilized. Duplicate if necessary.

19. Clean the bath during a shower. It is simpler working from within.

20. Keep work desk supplies in your briefcase, handbag, or vehicle for those eccentric deferrals and waiting periods.

21. Say 'no' more frequently and quit volunteering for everything.

22. Try not to continue rearranging paper. Handle each piece as it shows up.

23. Start your day before it dawns. Wake up early and plan your movements beginning of the day.

24. Try not to read passively. Search for new ideas. Use highlighters. Make short notes.

25. Try not to store magazines. Detach or photocopy the important part of the articles you will need.

26. Set a deadline for each project and endeavor to stick to it.

27. Always carry about a small jotter with you for note-taking.

28. Plan ahead of time your TV review time. It very well may be a continuous burglar.

29. Utilize hued names to signal significant dates in your arranging schedule and to feature earnest demands that surface.

30. Carry an inventory of Post-it Notes on your calendar.

31. Review your "junk mail" during your free time (for example, the last fifteen minutes of the day).

32. Take just lightweight suitcases while traveling via air. Delays can happen when hanging tight for your luggage to be cleared.

33. Utilize mostly transparent compartments for remains so you can see what you have in the fridge.

34. When leaving a message for somebody to get back to you, let them know the best time they can contact you.

35. If the individual you call isn't accessible, attempt to get the data you need from another person as opposed to leave a message.

36. Keep paper and pen helpful in each room.

37. Carry a versatile "Trident" 3-hole puncher in your folder case or meeting binder.

38. Record in your schedule the time by which you should go out (or hotel) If you have to attend any meeting at a far distance to get there in good time.

39. Have a lot of keys on you than you may think you will be needing.

40. Try not to be hooked on your phone. Utilize your answering machine to replying mail or voice messages, most especially to take messages during the supper hour or overlook the phone.

41. When masterminding doctor and dental specialist appointments, take the first slot of the morning so you can be quickly attended to and stay ahead of the crows at the hospital.

42. Keep a stock of welcome cards, stamps, and gifts close by.

43. Set away materials after use. Tidy up the mess as it's created.

44. Utilize a highlighter when reading letters and reports so you can check those parts requiring action.

45. Continuously check in with appointments; don't assume the fellow at the other end will remember.

46. Use stacking plate to sort mail as to charges, correspondence, garbage mail.

47. Spot shading dabs on the entirety of your charge cards for simple distinguishing proof.

48. Photocopy the two sides of your Mastercards (around nine for every page) and leave a duplicate in your home sheltered and safe storage box.

49. Utilize the driving time to tune in to tape tapes or CDs.

50. Record thoughts from tape tapes or CDs by managing them into a pocket recorder.

51. Keep a pocket recorder in your vehicle for chronicle thoughts, data, activities, and so on., as they strike you.

52. Buy into bulletins identified with your calling to eliminate understanding time.

53. Shading your different keys with little plastic rings, accessible in numerous stores, to avoid mishandling.

54. Photocopy birth certificates, marriage declarations, and so forth., and keep them in your documents.

55. Structure the habit for taking your arranging schedule with you any place you go – even in the midst of a get-away. You can record that ports-of-call, most loved cafés, lodgings, and individuals you meet.

56. Store void garments holders on one side of the storeroom and use it as required. Try not to give them a chance to blend with the ones being utilized.

57. Keep your personal belongings tote sack outfitted with every single personal thing, from the toothbrush to travel hairdryer, and use it only when you are about to go on a trip.

58. Discover approaches to delegate functions to people around you.

59. Keep your phone calls as short as possible.

60. Place a call through instead of chatting away for long hours.

CHAPTER FOURTEEN

THE ULTIMATE TOOL FOR DEALING WITH ANXIETY

Helen Keller was once asked, "Is there anything more terrible than being visually impaired?" She answered, "Yes. The most pitiable individual on the planet is somebody who has physical sight; however, he lacks vision." Ms. Keller was exceptionally discerning. Lots of people around the world have goals and dreams, yet like to sit and do nothing as opposed to masterminding out ways to achieve their goals. We have the ability to control our fate and reduce the pressures that life throws at us daily. The key to managing stress and reducing anxiety in our daily lives is, having objectives and following them determinedly enough to see them work out as intended. I didn't concur with Peter Thomas when he stated, "Achievement is the fulfillment of a foreordained objective; disappointment is non-attainment."

For whatever length of time, it takes for you to move toward your objectives, you are a success in my view. If you are moving the correct way, you will do well throughout everyday life. Inquire as to whether patients on mental wards have characterized objectives and know precisely what they truly desire. I figure you can envision what the appropriate response would be. Solicit the administrator from the power of a top-creating deal a similar inquiry. You will find that the best individuals in business, and throughout everyday life, practice objective setting as a customary piece of living.

In his book, Man's Search for Meaning, Victor Frankl, the successor of Sigmund Freud, contends that the "loss of expectation and mental fortitude can dangerously affect man." Because of his encounters in a Nazi concentration camp, Frankl argues that when a man never again has a thought process in living and no future to look toward, he twists up in a corner and bites the dust." Any endeavor to reestablish a man's internal quality in camp," he expresses, "had first to prevail with regards to demonstrating to him some future objective." I have no expectation of investing energy in a mental ward, yet I would like to be included as a high achiever throughout everyday life; it bodes well to set objectives as the victors do!

We live in a bustling world. Numerous individuals mistake stressful activity for achievement. A large number of us are so busy with life that we think that it's hard to stop for a while to consider such things as if we are making progress or just increasing our blood pressure. We can never make progress in existence without first thinking about where we need to go. We wouldn't head out on the sea, wanting to get someplace without having a specific course in mind. The understanding of the direction we need to take per time will help to reduce the stressful events around our lives and train us to have a calm and defined path in life.

Why Set Goals?

The FBI went into one town to research work by what had all the signs of being a sharpshooter. They were astonished to discover numerous bulls-eyes drawn on different focuses with shots that had entered the definite focal point of the objectives. At the point when they at long last found the man who had been doing the shooting, they asked him what his mystery was.

The best response was basic: he shot the slug first and drew the bull's-eye later. In application: Do we enable our exercises to decide our objectives, or do we have our goals to decide our exercises? A guard sticker peruses: "Try not to Follow Me, I'm Lost, Too." You can achieve a great deal throughout everyday life. Get your eyes on what you need. Try not to think about the explanation you can't have something. Concentrate in on how. Keep in mind what Warren Buffett said. Addressing a gathering of understudies, the wealthy person owned this expression about their capability to prevail throughout everyday life:

"Everyone here has the capacity totally to do anything I do and much past. Some of you will, and some of you won't. For the ones who won't, it will be because you get in your particular manner, not because the world doesn't permit you."

Ask yourself the "What if...?" question.

How might you answer a definitive "What if..." question:

If I needed to carry on with my life over, what might I do any other way?

Dr. Anthony Campolo, Professor of Sociology at Eastern College, St. Davids, Pennsylvania, shares the consequences of a review where 50 individuals 95 years and more established were asked: "If you could carry on with your life over what might you do any other way?" The appropriate responses astonished me. These older adults said that on the off chance that they could live their lives over, they would:

1. Reflect more.

These old people said they would reflect more on the important things while being grateful and strategize how to fix the things that aren't working out. The first section of this book has done clear justice in explaining what reflection/meditation is all about and the various ways we can apply it in our lives. Reflection helps you to consider what is happening in the present moment, and how to deal with your thoughts rather than suppressing it. It helps you ponder the importance of life, family, work, and significantly more.

2. Take the risk.

These great individuals said that they would have taken more risks throughout everyday life. On the off chance that they could re-live their lives, they wouldn't be so frightened to go for broke. They would have grown more fearlessness to wander out of their usual ranges of familiarity.

3. Accomplish things that would outlast them.

They needed to realize their lives meant something that long after they left this world; their effect would, in one way or another, live on. We, as a whole, can take in something from these individuals about defining objectives. Think about what they said as you set the course for your life.

Make your Heart's Desire dream list.

Escape from every one of the interruptions of life and pick a peaceful spot where you won't be interrupted. Finish the sentence at the highest point of the Heart's Desire Worksheet. It says, "If I had UNLIMITED cash, time, ability, capacities, and backing from my family, this is what I would do with my life..."

This is the best time to make your Dream List. Have your life partner, family, or kids around them out, as well – This will help you live a stress-free life, knowing that the most important people in your life are not left out. Creating this list brings so much calm because you somehow have a temporary blueprint to work with, and no matter what life throws at you, you can still keep your head above the waters. This will be an extraordinary time for your relationship. Unwind and let the thoughts immerse your mind. Try not to assess your potential for accomplishing everything you compose. What you write will energize you and move you. It might make you snicker. It will inspire you.

The majority of all, it will enable you to think about your Heart's Desire. Thoughts may come gradually from the outset; in any case, with determination, wavering will offer an approach to speed and energy. Your heart has wanted. Regardless of what anybody says, YOU CAN HAVE YOUR HEART'S DESIRES. You are not awful for needing to accomplish your goals. Wealth is something to be thankful for, and you deserve it. Achievement is for you. We all have Heart's Desires. The initial step of transforming those fantasies into the truth is to get those fantasies out before you where you can see and feel them.

Pick your major goal and move it to a goal card

From your Heart's Desire Worksheet, select the #1 most crucial goal. This is effectively controlled by asking, "Which goal captivates and energizes me the most?" Don't stress over whether you know precisely how to accomplish the goal now. Just choose which one is most significant and exciting to you.

At that point, write out this objective on a goal card. In Think and Grow Rich, Napoleon Hill pointed out that this was the mystery of the considerable number of men he met for the book. He found that, as a general rule, each well off individual he investigated had his primary objective composed on a 3x5 card. They conveyed their primary goals around, loose in their pockets, and read them frequently. So should you. Innumerable, a great many individuals who utilize this necessary procedure will vouch for its viability. I carry my card with me all over the place. I reserve my front right pocket for my main Goal. Nothing else ever goes in that pocket. Each time I put my hand in my pocket, think about what springs up on the screen of my mind? My main goal! Is it an awful thing to always have an image of goals on your mind? I think not.

Work out your main goal, consistently for 30 days.

A ground-breaking approach to prepare your "crew" is to work out your Heart's Desire Worksheet consistently for 30 days. This gives your "crew" a solid and exact request from you, the captain. The issue with numerous individuals is they stopped before the 'crew' has enlisted their request. Or then again more regrettable, the chief alters his perspective like every other minute. If you genuinely desire to affect, at that point, write on this sheet each day for 30 days. I guarantee you will be delightfully astonished.

CATEGORIES OF GOALS

Work Goals

What objectives would you like to reach in each area stated? Does a salary raise? Career promotion? Okay, prefer to win some honor or special award? Where do you see your profession going? OK, would you prefer to change your profession?

Financial

What amount of cash do you want? What will your financial balance or ventures resemble in the nearest future, say six months? OK, would you like to make a million dollars? Would you prefer to possess all the more land asses? What will your yearly salary be in five years? When will you fabricate the new wing down at the malignancy medical clinic?

Social

Which associations will you join? What will your social life resemble later on? Would you like to gain new business connections? OK, prefer to make upgrades around there? What sort of companion will you be to other people?

Physical

What state will your body be in one year from now right now? If you intend to get in shape – what amount of calories would you like to burn? What duration of time? Would you prefer to eat healthier meals? Would you prefer to have more energy and vitality? Starting your exercise routines soon? When? Where? Who will be your accountability partners?

Mental

In what capacity will you build up your mind? What might you want to adapt more than all else? Would you be able to think about individual books you might want to read or courses you might want to take? What will they be? Memory training through regular study of a specific topic? Want to learn to speak in public? Learning a new dialect?

Family

What might you want to change at home? It is safe to say that you are investing in quality time and creating strong bonds with your family? What objectives do you have for your family life? What trips, occasions, plans will make you more extravagant on the family side of life?

Spiritual

What part of your profound life will you create? Have you detected a specific vacancy that otherworldly advancement may comprehend? What will you do about it? What will your association be in profound associations?

Put your objective recorded as a hard copy and make it explicit.

To state that you need to be less anxious, wealthy, or happily married is, even more, a desire than a goal. For an objective to be successful, you should depict in detail what it will resemble. For example, if I set a goal to be a millionaire, I have to define that goal in quantifiable terms. What will my financial statement resemble? What vehicle will I drive? A few specialists state you ought to venture to depict the shade of the car.

Use what conduct researcher Dr. Robert Mager calls the "Daddy Test." Write the goal and state, "Daddy, come watch me ... (express the goal)." If Daddy would know exactly what you are doing, at that point, it finishes the Daddy Test. For instance, if you state, "Daddy, come watch me be a millionaire," Daddy would not know what that implies. If I revise the goal and state, "Daddy, come watch me pay money for another, red Rolls Royce," at that point, Daddy would know what I would do – subsequently, it is a composed goal.

NINE STEPS TO EFFECTIVE GOAL SETTING

• List the goals in order of priority.

Since you will have a few goals in a single folio or document, it will be useful for you to list from which classification this specific goal comes. You will be acquainted in the blink of an eye with the Goals Mastery Worksheet that will give a spot where you can compose this data. The Worksheets are incredibly indispensable assets to enable you to accomplish your goals. You will round out one for every one of your goals. You will be approached to choose one goal as your A1 goal. This is your need goal.

- **Put your goal recorded as a hard copy and make it understandable for all to see.**

To say, you need to live a stress-free life, rich or joyfully hitched is all the more a desire than a goal. To be compelling, you should depict in detail what it will resemble. If I set a goal to be a millionaire, I have to characterize that goal in quantifiable terms. What will my financial balance resemble? What vehicle will I drive? A few specialists state you ought to venture to portray the shade of the vehicle. Use what the researcher, Dr. Robert Mager, calls the "Daddy Test." Write the goal and state, "Daddy, come watch me ... (express the goal)." If Daddy would know precisely what you are doing, at that point, it finishes the Daddy Test.

For instance, if you say, "Daddy, come watch me be a millionaire," Daddy would not know precisely what that implies. If I rewrite the goal and say, "Daddy, come watch me pay money for another, red Rolls Royce," at that point, Daddy would know precisely what I would do – in this manner, it is a written goal.

- **Give it a Deadline.**

Deadlines regularly scare individuals from goal setting. Will I feel like a disappointment if I don't achieve my goal on schedule? Try not to stress, and it very well may be changed. Maybe the date isn't right, yet setting a deadline time provides a goal. Other than accomplishment cutoff times, think about separating the goal into smaller pieces and setting achievements. Achievements are markers en route that will enable you to keep tabs on your development.

If you set a goal to lose 25 lbs. in ten months, you could date a goal for every one of the ten months. In the first month, you ought to have dropped 2.5 lbs., the equivalent the second, third, etc. Is it accurate to say that it isn't simpler to separate it and set shorter cutoff times? Anybody can lose 2.5 lbs. in a month. If you separated it much further, it would mean you would lose not precisely a large portion of a pound seven days.

- **Identify the potential Success Blockers.**

You need to know the various barriers to your goals and how to overcome them if, indeed, you want to have a stress-free life. It is not enough to set goals; you should know what may impede those goals and create subsequent plans to overcome them. You would be advised to anticipate them! Anything beneficial in life will have a cost to pay and obstacles to prevail. Fruitful goal-setters recognize those potential issues first before they experience them. This places them in a lot more grounded situations to defeat them.

A year ago, I set a goal to lose 25 lbs. I thought about the Success Blockers, the obstacles that would endeavor to obstruct the accomplishment of my goal. For me, the deterrents to that goal are that I loathe exercise and love food. I travel frequently and invest my energy in beautiful inns. I'm not the kind of individual who can go on a plane throughout the night, get to my lodging at noon, and request a plate of mixed greens from room administration. This is considerably progressively troublesome when there are prime rib and cheesecake on a similar menu. That was a potential deterrent for me. Considering this early enabled me to arrange for how to deal with the hindrance when I looked at it. It didn't generally work! I'm a sucker for cheesecake.

- **Identify the assets you will require.**

The odds are, you will require the help of specific individuals to see your dreams come to pass. Who are they? In what capacity should you approach them? What would it be advisable for you to ask them? Is there an affiliation or association you could join? A few goals require the help of expert assistance. Thousands have halted unreasonable drinking with the assistance of the incredibly famous Alcoholics Anonymous Twelve-Step Program.

This step drives us to distinguish the individuals, spots, associations, and assets important to achieve incredible things throughout everyday life. (I found out that there is a ton of help accessible for the individuals who stop long enough to consider, shut-up long enough to hear, and humble themselves enough to ask questions.)

At the point when I initially started in this industry, a significant number of the "important influencers" in the training and public speaking business openly gave of their opportunity to support me. They were excited to help somebody who dared to look for help and to try the guidance they gave.

- ## List what advantages this goal will bring.

Each goal has a cost and requires a specific level of penance and diligent work. At the point when you list the advantages of the goal, you remain persuaded to stay with it.

- ## Include a useful arrangement.

Time management expert and author Harold Taylor say, "Try not to hope to accomplish your goals without sufficient arranging. Arranging moves things from where they are currently to where we need them to be later on. It interprets the goal without hesitation." Sit down with your everyday organizer and calendar when you work to achieve the goals on your list. Make an arrangement that is sensible given your circumstance, yet build up an activity plan — rundown the means in question and when you will chip away at them.

- ## Build-in accountability partners.

Have you attempted to accomplish a specific goal only to fail over again? You feel the goal is valid, and you might want to oversee it. However, you can't get through. To accomplish goals, make yourself accountable to somebody you regard. This step may appear to be outrageous and demanding, and it likely could be for individual goals, yet different purposes that are basic can be accomplished by utilizing this method, especially if you have experienced issues with specific pieces of the goal. If this goal is essential to you and you need assistance, discover somebody whom you regard, who isn't hesitant to go up against you, and who will genuinely hold you to your goals. You may get together week by week or month to month to audit your advancement. Accountability is a fundamental step to achieving your goals. It might be perhaps the hardest method to use; however, it produces results!

List what major moves you will make in the following 24 hours, week, and month. We call them Action Commitments.

This is the most vital part of goal setting. This will either bring you euphoria or dissatisfaction. If you set a goal and make no solid move to accomplish it, you will raise your disappointment levels. You will disappoint yourself with no closure. You have written a goal, thought about the deadline and considered the roadblocks you might face in trying to achieve your goal. You have recorded the aptitudes you should create and named individuals who will enable you to accomplish the goal. You have thought through every one of the advantages to achieving the goal, built up an organized system, and even made yourself accountable to a respectable figure, and YOU DO NOT ACT? Never!

No active student of The Millionaire Mindset will allow himself to be considered as a part of the piles of those with dead dreams, dead dreams brought about by idleness. This step might be the most significant of the whole number of steps listed here. It moves your past goal defining into goal accomplishment. Sounds much better, isn't that right? In the space given in the Worksheet, list what explicit moves you will make in the following 24 hours. You need to record all Action Commitments in your schedule, organizer, or day-clock. Do likewise for the next week and the following month.

What you do in the important days and weeks following your goal setting sessions represent the most significant square of time you have. In the first couple of weeks, you have the opportunity to profit by your relentless focus and energy, which has been demonstrated during the activity. The effective beginning of these exercises before the finish of the first week or month furnishes us with another increase in vitality, compelling us toward the accomplishment of the goal. Starting these exercises rouses us to proceed with the procedure until new and all the more dominant habits are created. Regardless of how pretentious your goal may be, the activity can and ought to be acted upon within the next 24 hours. Choosing to just go through fifteen minutes in perception can be an Action Commitment.

CHAPTER FIFTEEN

STRUGGLING WITH THE ZEIGARNIK EFFECT?

Bluma Wulfovna Zeigarnik (1901–1988) was a Soviet psychologist and psychiatrist who discovered unfinished tasks causing anxiety between people. "The Zeigarnik Effect is a tendency, according to Psychwiki, to encounter recurrent thoughts regarding a goal that was once followed and left incomplete.

Intrusive thoughts about a goal once achieved and left incomplete.

The automatic mechanism signals that a previous task was left unfinished to the conscious mind, which could be centered on new objectives. It seems to be human nature to finish what we are beginning to do and, if it is not done, we will encounter dissonance. "Finish What You Began For many people, anxiety stems from the constant feeling that there are still things left to do. You will go to bed at night, thinking about what was left unfinished rather than what you have accomplished. The mind will grab on to what is open-ended and not addressed, and then you will be taunted by negative self-talk about what remains to be done. The truth is you're never really able to finish all that has to be done. Once the "to-do list" is finished, another will pop up to take his place. But you can learn how to manage your self-talk, so you can take a different approach to the endless list of things to do.

Stop watching the clock.

The first significant move is stopping for a moment. Take your eyes off the clock and look at the long list of to-dos you've stacked up. What is on the list? Are all the things that you really need to do relevant for you? Take a moment to put things first. What matters most, and why? What is the least important, and why?

Reorder you're to-dodo list, so it's an ordered and prioritized list of what needs to be done instead of a random list of anything you need to do. You can use any criterion you like. You can decide that the easiest things should be of the highest priority as you can tackle them immediately. Or, on the other hand, you can give the highest priority to the harder things to get them over with. What matters is making a strategy. Have a methodology that makes sense to you to go through your list. The exercise in this section should be used over and over again for many days if you suffer from a sensation that time is fleeting, and you are not winning it.

Remember, adopting a new habit takes a minimum of twenty-one days. It is better for time management if you can do it for at least one month. It's tricky to get a grip on managing your personal and time-related issues. Each day new things are added. Many people may not "value" your desire to change your approach in your life, and may continue to add things to your already overflowing plate. You have to be the one to take responsibility and be consistent.

Step One

Make a list of the outstanding things that need to be managed. Start with a random list of what's on your to-do sheet right now.

Step two

Rearrange the list by priority order. Number the items 1 (most important) to 10 (lowest). If you have more than ten products, place these in priority order on a separate list. They have no more than ten for the purposes of this exercise.

Step 3

Review your list of 10 and see where you can break down steps into more discrete tasks. For example, if you need to move your aging mother to a nursing home, and you have this as one "to - do," instead recognize that there are multiple steps involved. There are probably ten or twelve things that you need to do before you can do that job. Take the item you want to do and identify each piece in the process so that you can see exactly what is involved. Often the to - do cycle is dissected, and you can see exactly what's involved. Dissecting the to - do and splitting it into smaller bits often can potentially change the order of priority. This is fine; if you need to change things around, then come up with a final list on which to work.

Step Four

Now take each of the pieces on the to-do list and write alongside them an assumed timeframe. How long do you take every step? What does it mean? At this stage, will to-do should have steps, and then related time frames. You may end up with a page for each to-do; place the pages on top with the most relevant one in priority order. For each of the to-dos, you may want to have a file folder, but be sure to code them by priority order, whichever system you use.

Step Five

Analysis now to see if there's something else you can assign to. Are there any bits others could do for you? What imaginative ways to achieve some of the items that are on the list?

Step Six

Then transfer the measures onto a calendar for the first three priority to-dos, along with their corresponding time frames. When are you going to be doing these things? What day? What time? What time? Who else will you join? Write them down. Check this every morning, or first thing, so you've got the strategy for the day.

Step 7

Now get your optimistic claims into the process. Every day you check your to-do list or write down your steps in your diary, you want to be aware of any negative self-talk that tells you it's "just too much to do," to be aware of any negative self-talk that tells you it's "just too much to do." I need to have at least one month of doing this.

"Time is a man-made creation. I'm in control of my time; it's not my duty." "I will say 'no' the next time anyone asks me to take it on if I don't believe I can do it. "Taking steps one at a time helps me to work through my to-do list and do something every single day." "I took the time to plan, prioritize, and break down steps. I know what's important and what I need to concentrate on." "I refuse to be pulled into confusion about what I need to do. I'm out of an anxious state, watching and making my plans." "I can do what I need to do. I focus on my goals." "I'm less productive in thinking about what I need to do and feeling anxiety. "I'm clear about what I need to do, and I do it." "I'm feeling good about what I do every day. I am in control of my life. 'You will benefit from practicing good time management in several ways. At work, you can become more successful, more productive at home, and less worried about what you need to do.

CHAPTER SIXTEEN

RELEASING STRESSORS

This chapter addressed a number of stress-related aspects. You may have previously assumed that stress was only a normal and common reaction to the problems of life, but now you've noticed the stress and anxiety visit in different ways. If tension controls your life, take a look at this chapter to determine which aspects you want to start practicing in order to become calmer, and which aspects you want to start practicing in order to become calmer and more at peace. When you live life under stressful overload, you are not as successful. For several different ways, you should replace the negative self-talk with more constructive strategies.

The Importance of Core Values

One of the challenges of modern living is to figure out what is really important and to differentiate those from the obligations that at first seem important but really don't matter when you take the time to examine them. If you're like most people, then you may find that reducing, coordinating, or bypassing the deluge of knowledge you routinely encounter becomes increasingly difficult. Today we have more knowledge, data, and material possessions at our fingertips than any previous generation, but this new way of life doesn't come with instructions on how to handle it. Many of us feel so overwhelmed we don't step back and evaluate the impact of overloading knowledge. Nor do we know how to make it a priority. Instead of consciously deciding what is best for us, we become reactors of what life throws upon us. No doubt, our ancestors and ancestors were as busy as we are. They didn't have the advantage of all the time-saving technologies to make their lives more efficient and simpler. But they had a big advantage over our generation — they weren't overwhelmed with the information stream and deluge of options we face every minute of the day.

They've been straightforward on how to allocate their time, with fewer resources and fewer options to entice or confuse. Those who grew up during the Great

Depression, the "Greatest Generation," had strong, clear values and priorities, and a solid sense of purpose forged during the difficult years during and after World War II. This generation of Americans has been defined by a strong work ethic coupled with a focus on family, faith, and patriotism. They understood who they were and what they stood for, and therefore how to concentrate their energies and time. Fortunately, there is an easy way to break through modern society's "noise," which will help you make good choices if you are confused by all the options available: identify your core values.

Why Values Core?

Defining your beliefs and guiding principles for your life is one of the best ways to remove the mental clutter and lead a more satisfying life. Now we need these concepts more than ever to help us understand how we want to invest our time, energy, and resources.

Why does it matter?

Since your core values can be a measuring stick for all your life decisions and choices, keeping you focused on the person you want to be and the life you want to live. You build the best atmosphere for happiness, inner peace, and positive thinking by living in harmony with your values. Core values form a foundation for your life that endures over time, challenges in life, and significant changes. Embracing your core beliefs is like becoming a tree with strong and stable roots — life storms won't let you down. You minimize uncertainty, overthink, stress, and anxiety when you're clear about your beliefs.

One of the main values Barrie has in her professional life, for example, is independence and versatility. She did not want to do a typical 9-to-5 job once she established this importance because she realized she wouldn't be content. It was quick to say, "No, thank you," even though great work opportunities came her way because she was consistent about her principles.

Personal development writer and author Steve Pavlina explain the importance of core values like this: Principles serve as our guide to put us back on track every day, so that day after day we step in the direction that brings us closer and closer to our vision of the "best" life we would be able to live. The "best" is your own ideal, but usually, when you get closer to this ideal, you will experience "great" shades of more optimistic shades even though you never achieve "best." And this makes sense because there are many outcomes in life on a spectrum. Living out of sync with your values or outgrowing your current values will throw you off course and help make you feel nervous and depressed. If your beliefs have not been established, your life may feel unbalanced or directionless, and you do not know why.

In this section, we are going over four strategies to define your core values and make smart decisions about your life responsibilities, so what you do on a daily basis matches those important items.

Strategy # 1: Identify YOUR core values

1. You need to have a strong grasp of what's right for you to understand why something feels wrong. How do you want to live your life, and who do you want to be? You're sailing the sea of life without a compass if you've never established your values. You allow the winds and storms to define your direction and unquestionably accept the result. Even if you've defined them in the past, revisiting them doesn't hurt, because your values can change over time.

2. Here's a cycle of 6 steps to describe your beliefs.
1. First, go through this list of words of value on Barrie's Live Bold and Bloom blog, and write down any word of value that you feel is important to your personal life.
2. Go through the list again, then write down any word of importance that feels important to your career or company.

3.   Select the top five to six values for both lists, and write them down on two different sheets of paper. Label one "Values of Life" pad, and the other "Values of Work."

4.   List all the ways you actually live out of harmony with the value under increasing value. For example, if quality time with family is one of your values, but you travel five days a week, you may not be honoring that value.

5.   Think about actions you could take to fix those situations of out-of-alignment for each value. Ask yourself, "What do I have to do to rectify this situation, so I honor my core values? "If you use the family time example, maybe one action would minimize your travel schedule or hire some household tasks while you're at home so you can spend more quality time with your family. Write these down for both life and work even though the acts now seem unlikely.

6.   Place a checkmark next to the things that are doable for you now or in the near future on both lists of things. Break down these actions into much smaller, easier to handle acts. Such activities may include making calls, rearranging your schedule, delegating certain tasks, brainstorming a potential career change, talking about opportunities to re-engage with your partner, etc. Once you have a list of principles that fit with your priorities, revisit it on a regular basis to make sure that the activities you take reflect those desired outcomes. You may want to reflect on your personal values first, and then your professional values. Or you could pick one value from each and start there.

Whatever you choose, be sure to start with your area of life where you feel the biggest disconnect. It is here that you possibly experience the most inner pain and mental tension. Chip away from your regular action plan, so that you can establish improvements and guidelines that will keep you from moving away from your beliefs. Even small, gradual changes in your attitude can produce a big, positive shift. You're going to have a sense of direction and an intent that feels real to you, even if you can't instantly act upon it. This attitude is extremely inspiring! There will always be periods of change and turmoil, but this lesson in principles gives you the tools to work through all the ups and downs of life.

Strategy # 2: Explain Your Life Priorities

- Once you have set your core values, use this knowledge to complete another exercise that will enrich your life — clarify your life priorities, so you know exactly how to spend your time, energy, and money. We allow the demands of life to decide our actions and decisions without knowing our goals. An email is coming in, and we are answering. Our Facebook page offers an attractive bid, and we buy it. Someone interrupts the flow of our work, and we allow that. There are no rules, no guidelines, no goals to help us when we don't know the bigger "why" of our lives. Here's another exercise that we suggest to help you find out where you're investing your time, energy, and money right now. Respond as honestly as possible the question below. (Also, make sure your list of core personal and professional values is handy when you answer.)

- How much time per day do you feel you are spending on things that are contrary to your core values (i.e., surfing the net, watching boring TV, shopping, or working in a job you hate)?

- How do you unconsciously invest the money?

- How do you communicate with those people you unconsciously care about?

- How do you make career decisions (i.e., have a predetermined strategy, or spend most of your day in "reaction mode")?

- How much time do you spend thinking about how your time and money should be best spent?

- What roles, responsibilities, and relationships do you unconsciously allow for in your life?

- How do you ignore other essential parts of your life, for which you never seem to have time?

Now that you are seeing how you are currently investing your time and attention let's decide the perfect way you want to prioritize your life's important areas. For the sake of this topic, let's look at seven key areas of life to help you set your goals and how you would like to invest your time and money. If you want any of these areas to be added or deleted, please feel free to do so if they do not apply now.

The scopes are

1. Carrier
2.   Friends.
3. Marriage (or sharing in love)
4. Spiritual / personal growth / self-improvement
5. Leisure
6. Managing life (i.e., homework, financial planning, budgeting, etc.)
7. Health and wellness That leaves 16 waking hours if you sleep 8 hours a day. Let's take away for personal hygiene practices and feeding 2 hours a day. That leaves 14 hours of walking a day, or 98 hours a week. Let's round that up to 100 hours a week for convenience.

How would you prioritize those seven core areas of your life in an ideal world? How many hours would you prefer to devote to each area (using your values to guide you) of those 100 per week? Two examples;

The main interests of Barrie's life center heavily on work, love relationships, and life management. Her children are young adults, and many of her friends and family are not nearby since she recently relocated to a new area. Ideally, she would like to devote more time to leisure and social events, health, and self-improvement. As she gets more acclimatized to her new location, she tries to focus more on those things. Owing to his recent marriage, the birth of his son, and the fact that his parents had just turned 70, Steve's main concern is heavily focused on the family. So his new goal is to spend as much time as possible with the people he most loves in the world. Although his career (i.e., online business) and fitness were the top priorities just a couple of years ago, they are no less important than his interpersonal relations. This also means "letting go" of the big objectives that once seemed significant. And though he still likes to work hard, if he can't reach a goal related to business or his health, he has learned not to feel nervous.

Now from the writers, these are only two examples. To help you define your goals, we suggest that you answer two basic questions:

1. How different is the truth of your present life goal from your ideal?

2. What are certain acts that you need to take to reflect on what really matters to you?

We suggest that you start with the goal that will make the most of your life or where you feel the most imbalance. You may find that this area represents one or more of your values, which you don't respect. For example, you may have a core family-related interest and a life-priority to spend more time with your family. Start small by agreeing to add an additional hour a week to spend quality time with your family. This will, of course, bump out any other task, but you also bump out something that can easily be bumped out — or at least something that is not a major priority. Continue to add weekly time to your life goals before you have them rearranged to match your ideal closer. Changing a priority can be tricky sometimes. If you want to spend more time with your kids, is your work schedule going to affect that? If so, what would you do to handle the consequences? If you want to concentrate more on your health and wellbeing, you're going to have to build new and demanding behaviors to ensure that you carry this goal through.

If you want a safe, happy life, you may have to give up time in front of the television or on the phone, which might be hard at first. It's not enough simply to state your goals in life. You have to take the often tough steps required to make the changes in your life that you want to see. But the more you get to your goal, the less you'll experience internal tension and struggle. Over time, you're not going to miss those old patterns, decisions, and behaviors — and your life is going to work more naturally because you're living authentically, true to your principles.

Strategy # 3a: Emphasis on Positive Goal Setting

A natural consequence of having principles and setting goals is to understand how these can contribute to your future life. Although thinking about the future leads to an unsettled mind, preparing for the future is a beneficial and necessary practice that can set the stage for true fulfillment in the years ahead. But can you really look to a better future, and yet be content with your life right now? Can you be happy and, at the same time, evolve? We assume concentrating on the future is possible while also learning how to appreciate the present moment. In the present moment, there are many great authors and metaphysical thinkers who talk of contentment. The renowned psychologist Abraham Maslow reminds us that "the ability to be in the present moment is a major component of mental well-being." Thích Nhat Hanh, the Zen Buddhist monk and bestselling author, advises that every moment in your life, every breath, every move you take, should be perceived consciously as a moment of joyful coming. He says that when you're happy, you don't have to wait for improvement, for anything better, for the future. If you want to see all the success and goodness around you in the present moment, you will be happy right now.

This is easier said than done, of course.

The complexities of our daily lives continually drag us into the future. We're worried about paying the bills, how our kids will turn out if we'll stay healthy. And the very nature of targets being set is forward-looking. Longing and battling "what is" causes pain. Wishing for more, for something special, for something better in the moment, at the cost of contentment, robs us of our lives. If that's the case if they take you away from the moment, why should you concentrate on your future goals? And you'll undergo change and transition whether or not you want to reflect on it. Change is a constant of life, whether we remain in the moment relaxed lotus pose or wring our hands over some possible potential outcome. And we should be conscious about building our future as well. When you accept the fact that contentment and progress will occur at the same time, you lower the stress of believing it's either a plan or a proposition. There is a way to strike a balance between self-creation and mindfulness.

The cycle of developing and achieving your goals can be seen as a place of happiness and contentment. Instead of holding back happiness while awaiting a result, enjoy every step along the way. We will savor and celebrate every discovery, every small action against your goals. Knowing that setting goals isn't incompatible with being conscious, let's explore how to build and work towards your goals in a way that supports your life's bigger "why." When you first sit down to contemplate your future goals, remember to make reference points for your core values and life preferences handy. As long as your values and priorities remain valid, they should be the compass in which to direct your objectives. Otherwise, you're setting yourself up for a future of disappointment and dissatisfaction. In the next part, we'll go over the method Steve uses to create simple goals that concentrate on what really matters. The benefit of this approach is that you will feel less stressed about the future, and instead concentrate on what is going on in your life at the moment.

Strategy # 3b: Build Quarterly S.M.A.R.T. Goals

The simplest way to concentrate on what is really important in life is to reach S.M.A.R.T. goals in the immediate future. This means you're setting goals for each quarter (i.e., three months) rather than the year-long goals that often take you out of the moment. Let's begin with a simple definition of S.M.A.R.T. objectives: George Doran first used the acronym S.M.A.R.T. in the November 1981 issue of the Management Review. It stands for the following: S pecific, M easurable, A ttainable, R elevant, and T imebound. S: Specific targets answer your six "W" questions: who, what, where, where, what, and why.

When you are able to identify each feature, you'll know the resources (and actions) are needed to achieve a goal.

- Who: Who participates?

- What: What is it that you want to achieve?
- Where: Where to finish the goal?
- Where: When would you like to do it?
- What: What criteria and restrictions could harm you?
- For what: Why are you doing this?
- ❖ S: Specificity is crucial because when you hit these milestones (date, place, and target), you'll know you've accomplished your target for certain.
- ❖ M: Measurable objectives are described with specific times, quantities, or other units — essentially anything that measures progress toward an objective. Setting tangible goals makes it easy to assess whether you have made progress from point A to point B. Measurable goals also help you figure out when and when you are heading in the right direction.
- ❖ A: tangible target statement usually addresses questions beginning with "how," such as "how much," "how many," and "how fast." A: Attainable goals push the boundaries of what you think is feasible. While not difficult to complete, they are always daunting and full of hurdles. The trick to achieving an attainable target is to look at your present life and set a goal that seems slightly beyond your grasp. That way, you still achieve something of importance, even if you fail.
- ❖ R: Relevant Targets are based on what you really want. They are the exact opposite of objectives that are contradictory or dispersed. From success in your career to happiness with the ones you love, they are in harmony with all that is important in your life.
- ❖ T: Time-bound milestones have different timescales. Within a goal date, you are supposed to get the desired result. Time-bound goals are demanding and ground-breaking. You can set your target date for today, or you can set your target date for a few months, weeks, or years from now. The trick to achieving a time-bound target is setting a deadline that you can reach by working backward and forming patterns (more on that later).

The aims of the S.M.A.R.T. are straightforward and well established. The result you want to achieve is in no doubt. You'll know at the end whether you've or haven't reached a common target. For starters, here are S.M.A.R.T. goals pertaining to the seven areas of your life we listed in the previous section:

1. Career: "I will acquire five new projects within two months for my Web design agency through referrals, networking, and social media marketing campaigns."

2. Family: "By taking them for a holiday at least once every six months, I can reinforce my relationship with my children. This can be done by setting aside one hour per month during my analysis session and preparing potential ideas for the trip. Love (or enjoy partnership): "Friday night, I'll define three things I really enjoy about my wife, and tell her about them. This will be done by scheduling a block of 30 minutes on Tuesday so that I can recall all the good times we had together. "

3. Spiritual / personal growth/self-improvement: "I'm going to take five minutes every day to thank for all that's positive in my life. I can build the habit by setting aside time to remember what's important right before lunch. "

4. Leisure / social: "I'm going to spend three hours per week studying and practicing painting in watercolor. This is achieved by removing unimportant customs such as watching TV. "

5. Life management: "Through my 401k, I will save 10 percent of each paycheck and invest it in index funds." Health and fitness: "I'm going to work out at least 30 minutes per day, three days a week by December 31." Hopefully, these seven examples will give you an idea of how to create S.M.A.R.T. goals that will lead to a life of balance. Now let's go through a cycle of six steps that will turn this knowledge into practice.

Step # 1: Define What's Important to You

The trick to achieving realistic goals isn't to concentrate on all your life areas. The explanation is simple: if you want to find purpose in what you are doing, you will easily feel exhausted if your days are set on a target laundry list. Yeah, forward-thinking is necessary, but you do want to have enough time to live in the present moment. Our advice is to reflect on your life's three or four regions. You will do this by looking at the seven fields we addressed and deciding what is actually most important to you. Simply build expectations from there and turn into a result, you find both daunting and exciting.

Step # 2: Focus on Three-Month Goals

It was Steve's experience that long-term goals shift constantly. Very often, what seems urgent today is not necessarily next month. So the approach that works for him is to take the most important goals of his life and then break them down into three-month (or quarterly) objectives.

Why do you concentrate on the targets for three months?

Since your life is fast-paced and ever-changing, to keep up with all of these changes, it is always easier to set short-term targets as this helps to sustain continuous commitment and a high degree of motivation. Steve's experience has also been that long-term targets (i.e., anything beyond six months) are also demotivating. It's easy to procrastinate on clear action when you know a result is months away. You keep putting off your goals, hoping that next week you will focus on them. Next thing that you remember, it's been a year since, and nothing has been done. So, to keep it straightforward, we suggest defining the three or four areas of your life that are most important or you right now, and then establishing a clear S.M.A.R.T. goal for each one that you plan to reach over the next three months.

Step # 3: Use a Weekly Review to create a Schedule

When you have a dozen other obligations, it's not always easy to work consistently on your goals. Fortunately, there is a simple solution to this dilemma — schedule a weekly review session in which you will be creating a daily action plan for the next seven days. The weekly review is a great concept taught by David Allen at Getting Things Done. It is a straightforward operation. Once a week (Steve likes Sundays), take a look at the next seven days, and plan the activities/projects that you would like to do.

All of this can be accomplished with three basic steps:

1. **Answer three questions:** observe the next seven days carefully and answer these three questions: What are my personal obligations? What are my projects priority? How long do I have? Your answers to these questions are extremely significant because they will decide how much time you will devote to your goals for the next seven days. The lesson here is you shouldn't have hundreds of events planned for your week. That is the best way to live a mentally cluttered life. Instead, it's easier to consider a fair amount of time ahead of time that can be dedicated to your important goals.

2. **Schedule project tasks:** Plan out the next seven days after answering these three questions. The best way to do so is to look at the list of the most relevant tasks for each target and plan time to follow up.

3. **The system captured ideas:** If you're like Barrie and Steve, then you've probably got loads of brilliant ideas for your goals every week. The problem is, how is it that you follow them up? My recommendation is to process those reports, make one of two choices:

1) take immediate action on them or

2) plan a date when you are going to follow them up. Here's how it would work: If the idea is actionable ... then write a step-by-step plan about how you're going to do it. Only write down a series of steps that you're going to take on this idea and then plan those ideas into your week. If the idea is NOT actionable ... then bring the idea into a monthly checked archive tab. When you are doing this with every idea you have, you are not going to fail to follow up at the right time. The weekly analysis is a vital part of making your goals come true. When you prepare each week, you build a sense of urgency, which makes it more likely that you will be following up on each goal. The weekly analysis will also help you build a schedule that you can convert into a regular task list.

Step # 4: Take action on your goals.

Without action, it is difficult to attain your goals. In reality, the trick to get what you want is to arrange time into your week that is devoted exclusively to your objectives. That's why we suggest the following actions: convert your aim into a project: Starting at the target date and working your way backward is the best way to do so. Visualize how to hit that goal. Which are the practical steps you have taken to get to this point? Once the acts are established, you simply place them in a simple, step-by-step list.

- ❖ Schedule time to focus on goals: How much time you spend on each goal depends on what each task needs. Many tasks may require only a few minutes per week, while others require hours of your day (that's why it's important to consider per goal's time commitment). Consider how much time you're going to need for every job, and plan it into your week.
- ❖ Transform priorities into priority tasks: We all have those busy schedules full of overlapping activities. The answer, right? Start your day with first thing in the morning working on goals, or any other time when you're feeling the most energy.
- ❖ Timing of single actions: Many people get bogged down by single actions that are important but not urgent immediately. A simple remedy for that is to schedule a number of single acts each week.

Step # 5: Revisit Your Goals

The secret to doing everything in life is consistency. (For more on how to do that in ToDoist, here's a detailed guide they put together that will help you through the whole process. That's why you should daily review your "goal project" and make sure you hit every important milestone. We suggest that you establish precise metrics for each step of the process and use a weekly analysis to ensure you are always working on those. The setting aside of time for a regular analysis is a crucial step towards achieving every objective. It doesn't matter how busy you are — if you don't check your goals every day, you'll have less chance of succeeding.

The fact is, life will often throw big curveballs on the pursuit of a long-term target. Such tasks can also be frustrating and cause you to feel less optimistic about an objective. Our advice is therefore simple: Check your goals at least two to three times a day. That way, you will keep them at the forefront of your mind and remind yourself why you regularly take a specific action.

Step # 6: Review your quarterly targets, which you work hard every day. You also take a weekly and regular look at them. The Issue? Many people never step back and consider the "why" behind every single target. In other words, people don't study their priorities to see if they really are worth following. That's why reviewing your goals every three months is vital, making sure they are consistent with your life intent, and then developing new goals based on what you've learned. You will complete this evaluation by answering a variety of questions:

- Did I produce the desired result?
- Which were positive tactics and unsuccessful ones?
- Have I made 100 percent of my efforts to achieve these goals?
- If not, then why not?
- Did I achieve results that are compatible with my efforts?
- Will I set a similar goal for next quarter?
- What targets will I alter or eliminate?
- Was there anything different which I would like to try?

While completing this assessment takes a few hours, you should still take the time to do it every quarter. This would be your greatest defense against spending time on a target that is not consistent with your goals for the long term. So, it was a brief introduction to the importance of setting targets for S.M.A.R.T. Now, the best way to ensure that you are really setting goals you really want is to associate them with a personal passion. We'll show you how to do this inside the next (and final) approach.

Strategy # 4: Align Ambitions with Your Interests

Too many people are living a life of quiet desperation. They wake up with a sensation of dread, anxiety, or sadness at low levels. At work, they feel underused, undervalued, and underwhelmed. And when they get home, they feel drained mentally and physically, with only enough strength to take care of the kids, cook dinner, and plop onto the couch to watch television for a few hours. Then they wake up and do it again. Even if that doesn't exactly define you, I'm sure you can relate. We're all slipping into the occasional rut. We agree inferior to our dreams. We are remaining in jobs that do not encourage us or make us happy. All this angst adds to our stress and mental clutter.

Life has a way to swallow us up, and we're far down a road before we know it, that feels nothing like who we are or what we want for our lives. When we know this, we have commitments and duties; this gives yet another justification to stick to the status quo — even if we dislike it. Although the idea of "finding your passion" may remind you of those woo-woo quotes you often see on Facebook or Instagram, balancing what you do on a daily basis with goals you believe are genuinely important is still incredibly important.

The truth is that when you feel unfulfilled in your job, your mental health can be negatively impacted. Think about how much negative mental resources you have given to a poor boss, a job that you dislike, or a career that you regret. We're spending big chunks of our lives working, and the decision you make about your career will make or break your overall happiness.

If you find work you love, not only will you free your mind from oppressive thoughts, but you will feel energized in all areas of your life as well. And what does living out your passion mean? In a few examples, we think it can be defined:

- Most days, you wake up feeling excited and positive about what you've been doing that day.
- You feel like you're in the "right" place, doing something that feels authentic to who you are and how you're wired in your job or life.
- You bring in your life and work interesting, like-minded people.

- You feel comfortable and excited about what you're doing because it's a perfect match for you.
- You experience a greater function or meaning-or at least you are more commonly fulfilled.
- Your life as a whole is better, and your relationships are healthier, as you are happier, more self-directed, and more involved in your work.

It's not like teaching you how to follow a recipe or change the oil in your car, it's not like finding your passion and making it part of your life that happens overnight, and it's not an exact "paint by numbers process." To work it out, it means a number of behavior and tests. In reality, in her online course Path to Passion, and in her book The 52-Week Life Passion Project, Barrie teaches the cycle.

Anybody reading this book is exceptional. We also have various personalities, talents, aspirations, and responsibilities to live. What you consider to be your passion will be different from what others find to be. So, that's why we suggest that you use a 14-step exercise to discover your passion.

Stage 1: Vision-write.

Write down what you want in every area of your life-particularly in your work-using your values and goals as guides. You do not know exactly what to include, but to explain what you don't like is a good starting point. For starters, when Barrie wrote her dream of life five years ago, it looked like this: I live in an interesting, progressive, vibrant city where I can enjoy nature, the arts, culture, great food, and people with likeminded. I work in a profession that I enjoy, where I support others and use my coaching and leadership skills, as well as my writing and artistic abilities. My job is versatile, which gives me flexibility from anywhere to move and work.

My income keeps that, but I don't allow my job to create an imbalance in my life. I am in a relationship with a smart, talented, funny, caring, and ethical man who is loving, respectful, and mutually supportive. I have a network of close and supportive friends and family with whom I spend time regularly, and I have a caring, positive relationship with each of my three young adult kids. I also spend time in nature and travel many times a year to new locations. With each year, I remain interested, healthy, and health-conscious, and I remain open to new ideas and possibilities for my life. She can honestly say that by moving to a new city, building an online business related to personal development and helping others, going on several amazing trips, and nurturing their relationships, health, and freedom, she has made this vision a reality. Our recommendation is to write down what you want, and then revise it when you recognize something you do/don't want in your life. Finally, post your dream every day so you can see it.

Phase 2: Revise your daily life.

If you're feeling too focused on what you don't like about your life, then take a look at your current life to see how much of it matches the previous exercise's vision. You want to keep those stuff running, and remember that part of your dream already happens for you ... right now! Write a list of everything things you like or see as good about your work — whether it's the comfy desk chair or the client that you really want. For your personal life, compose the same list containing everything in your life that fits well for you. When you're finding your passion, don't throw the baby out with the bathwater. Often, because we're so focused on the negative, we forget good stuff in our lives. If you are interested in learning more about this subject, then read this blog post about careful journaling that will help you identify potential passions you might be missing right now.

Step 3: Focus on yourself.

Start to learn more about who you are, what motivates you, and what abilities you possess. Take online personality evaluations such as The Myers Briggs Test The Keirsey Temperament Sorter Or strengths evaluation tests such as Strengths Finder 2.0 or this free online strengths test Know what you can about your personality style. Finding knowledge about you, you will discover, gives you a sense of self-awareness that is both soothing and enlightening.

Stage 4: Keep training.

Set aside 10 minutes a day to read everything that you can about your future passion, interests, or ideas. Look at how those passions and thoughts were turned into professions by others. Take notes of something that you think is important or significant. For a potential hobby, you can also consider taking an online course to acquire more in-depth information and understanding of what you are researching.

Stage 5: Quest closer.

You may find one or more career options that jump out at you as you begin reading and researching. Conduct more research on these topics to find out exactly what kind of training or education is required, who is already effective in this field, what kind of salary you might receive, and how long it will take to become competent in this field. Begin filling in the blanks with all the necessary information to make this potential passion a reality for you and the framework of your life.

Step 6: Locate a mentor.

Find one or two people who do whatever you want to do and do it well. Check them out. Give them emails asking if they can get advice. Make a list of any questions you would like to know.

Phase 7: And write and brainstorm.

Think of all the moves you need to take to push the needle to live your passion (once you've done your research). Create a long list of acts, then go back and make a list a priority and order. Bridge every move to the smallest possible measure.

Step 8: Make the first move.

To get the ball rolling towards your passion, do one specific thing. Perhaps it's getting your resume in order, signing up for a training class, or contacting someone else. You may not feel 100 percent confident this first step is the right one, but to find out, you must take it. So, set and take a date. Refer back to the previous approach on setting quarterly goals for S.M.A.R.T. if you get stuck. We suggest that your pursuit of a successful career be turned into a project where you take regular action.

Step 9: Determine what drive to test.

One of the easiest ways of finding out whether a passion is really a passion is to try it out. Rather than committing yourself completely to a new job or starting a company, find a way to gain hands-on experience by volunteering, a part-time job, or even shadowing someone for a few days. This test drive offers real-world input to help you determine if you have really found what you love.

Step 10: Comment on others.

Mind keeping those concerned close to you and in the loop. You will potentially come up against some opposition. Think ahead about this possibility, and how you are going to deal with it. What do you think is the bottom line? For them? Hold the Communication Lines open.

Step 11: Save Money.

Start putting back money into a savings account. It could be important when you make a transition to something different. It may be used for additional education or training, starting a company, or financially supporting you as you get a business up and running. Start talking about how you might put in a pinch of extra cash. Especially if you are moving from one full-time job to another, getting a contingency plan is still a positive idea.

Phase 12: Revenue planning.

Determine your annual income that is reasonable least. To do this, you need to know how you're spending your money, where you can (and willing to) cut back, and how long you're able to stay at this level of income. You don't want to go into debt, so that needs to be a reasonable amount that can support a lifestyle of basics.

One great way to track your spending and keep up with your finances is the Mint app. To get a full picture of your financial position, you can enter your billing records, current debt, and bank accounts here. You can then use Mint to completely understand how much money you need every month.

Phase 13: Take on your current work.

Be sure to include how you can switch from your current job into your new one as part of your action measures. Will you continue to work in your old job when you launch your new job? How and when are you going to discuss that with your employer? Make sure you leave on a good note and handle things professionally so you can keep those ties together.

Step 14: Stay action, motivated.

It's normal to feel a lot of fear when going from something safe and stable into the unknown. Thinking, organizing, fretting, and pontificating only go so far, and they add to your mental humiliation. Oriented behavior will move you forward every day. If you don't know what to do, then simply do something. Take one small step to make your dream come true.

Some of the beneficial outcomes of this 14-step process are that when you regain control of your life and move toward something more meaningful, you build a sense of intent. The desire to work for your goal is often just as rewarding as a result. Greg Johnson, author of Living Life on Purpose: A Guide to Creating a Life of Excellence and Importance, says, "Focus on the road, not the destination. Joy is not found in completing an operation but in doing it. "Much of our mental illness and pessimistic thought stems from feeling insecure about our lives and being out of control. You will have more and more mental clarity and peace of mind until you start taking steps to pursue your passion. Okay, you've learned a variety of techniques at this stage that you can use to resolve your negative thinking habits and that the effect of life responsibilities that just don't matter. We'll talk about the negative effects that certain relationships have on your mental well-being in the next segment, and what to do about it.

CHAPTER SEVENTEEN

CLEAN UP YOUR LIFE AND REDUCE STRESS

Up until this point, we have just covered how to effectively get rid of anxiety, set goals, avoid procrastination by managing your time and, managing the use of the physical or electronic spaces. You can likewise have clutter in the psychological, social, and media aspects of your life. This mess can be significantly harder to manage, on the grounds that it is difficult to distinguish. It isn't something you see, yet something you feel. In some cases, you may not understand that you are feeling cluttered. Frequently, life challenges result in stress and anxiety. At times, it can lead to outrage, discouragement, and other severe mental health conditions. In this chapter, I will be discussing tips and directions for reducing the clutters and mess around your life and managing the impacts of clutter on your feelings and mental capacities.

MANAGING MENTAL CLUTTER

Are you familiar with that feeling of being physically depleted yet having a racing mind when you rest for the evening? That is a side effect of mental stress. The failure to unwind or to focus on a single task regularly arises because you have a variety of thoughts going on in your mind. Most individuals can't just push their concerns and duties aside. However, there are a few things you can do to manage these issues and develop a more useful mindset toward life.

UNWINDING TECHNIQUES

One of the essential unwinding systems is deep breathing. When you become overwhelmed or restless, your breathing increases. This increases your heart rate and blood pressure beyond the standard range. Pausing for a minute to focus exclusively on your breathing to return it to a moderate, rhythmical example quiets the battle-or-flight response in your body and will assist you with thinking about issues more objectively.

Exercise is an approach to use to erase anxiety and relaxing the mind. Short and incredible strolls, two or three steps down the stairs, a few stretch exercises, or a run on the treadmill are altogether extraordinary approaches to diminish stress. Include some music through earphones also, an MP3 player to help divert your mind from the stressful issues or thoughts involving the all-important focal point. For a quick mental escape from any area, work on envisioning symbolism. Envision a tranquil spot utilizing the entirety of your senses. Consider what it looks like, sounds feels tastes and scents. Using a place you realize well can help bring it reasonably to mind, and thinking on the entirety of the sensations will take your mind away from the present errand and give a relieving mental break.

There are numerous approaches to achieve a calm or quiet attitude. I, for one, discover online or phone games like Bubble Pop soothe my mind and relieve me of anxiety. My significant other likes to vent to a friend or relative as an approach to get the psychological wrinkles out, and one woman I know finds a hot cup of tea and a couple of calm minutes to be the ideal cure to a distressing evening.

FIGURE OUT HOW TO LET GO

Sometimes, mental mess emerges on the grounds that we hold the entirety of our duties close to our chest. Regularly, we can delegate a portion of our undertakings to other people or request help. It very well may be hard to relinquish work or then again commitments, however over submitting is awful for you and awful for the individuals you are attempting to help. Figure out how to designate suitable errands and trust skilled individuals to deal with them. You can likewise delegate in your home and public activity.

Try not to gobble up each volunteer opportunity that comes to your direction, and encourage the children to take up some of the duties around the home. By enabling individuals to help, you free yourself up to give quality time and exertion to errands that you can't delegate.

SINGLE-TASKING

The fast-paced universe of today has made everybody a multitasker. As a business owner, I frequently observed candidates list performing multiple tasks as one of their qualities, likely on the grounds that it was a catchphrase that they thought propelled certainty. While performing various tasks is undoubtedly fundamental in numerous parts of life, there are times when you have to close out the noise and focus on the job at hand. Permitting the weight of your daily to-do list to interfere with work, play, or different exercises can reduce your profitability or happiness.

CONNECT WITH NATURE

The natural world gives a lot of thoughts on the best way to carry on with a less jumbled life. Getting out into the world and making the most of its lovely sights and sounds is additionally an extraordinary method to clear your brain and separate yourself from incredible messiness, relieving stress in the long run. Go on a short stroll in the recreation center, take an evening climb or bicycle ride, or escape to a weekend getaway to enjoy yourself in the tropics.

CLEAN UP YOUR SOCIAL LIFE

An exorbitantly bustling social life can be the most optimized plan of attack on mental stress. I am definitely not recommending that you become a recluse or create antisocial habits, yet I do think there is something to be said for balance in every way. Investigate your day organizer or schedule. If the days are just twirls of ink and penciled-in errands, it is conceivable your week is cluttered beyond reasoning. If you try not to have a schedule or organizer, at that point, you may have a jumbled public activity without acknowledging it.

KEEPING A CALENDAR

One of the initial phases in cleaning up your social life is getting an obvious take a gander at your exercises. You don't have to spend too much on a costly cowhide organizer, be that as it may, acquiring a sensibly evaluated pocket schedule or organizer is a decent thought. I find that purchasing a little organizer in August is the best strategy. School organizers make flawless life organizers, and you can, for the most part, locate a quality thing during the school year kickoff season for somewhere in the range of $3 and $10. Organizers are an individual decision, so you should explore different avenues regarding what works best for you. I like a little book that incorporates any event five lines for each day of the week. I additionally favor that the organizer is as of now filled in with months also, dates since I have steady issues with filling them in myself. A companion who ministers a little church likes to utilize the electronic organizer in his cell phone. He should make on-the-spot responsibilities and discovered he would not generally have his organizer with him.

After twofold or triple-booking his time on a few events, he began recording everything on his telephone. The included advantage is that the phone gives a caution ring for every arrangement.

Discover a strategy for calendaring that works for you.

My mom utilizes a basic divider schedule on the cooler to record arrangements and significant dates. I use a more nitty-gritty organizer to monitor arrangements, get-togethers, due dates on employments, and then some. The key is consistency.

Figure out how to Say No When you take a look at your timetable in an organizer or schedule, you will perceive how occupied you genuinely are. If there is little room to compose whatever else in a given week, you may need to reduce a portion of your social commitment. Numerous individuals have a habit to never disapprove of things. They try not to need to pass up great occasions, social climbing, organizing, or significant employments. A decent companion is partial to stating, "Individuals consistently state they don't have sufficient opportunity. All things considered, everybody has the same sum. Everybody has 24 hours consistently."

The way to diminishing social clutter isn't increasing the additional time. It is organizing your time suitably, and that implies figuring out how to say no. If the family has been in a hurry all week, disapprove of the Friday supper greeting so everybody can get some required personal time. Make it a point to spend a specific number of nighttimes inconsistently at home and timetable the different nighttimes cautiously. You ought to continuously be charitable when declining solicitations and attempt to abstain from turning the same companions as the week progressed. In any case, if a companion can't comprehend that you are worn out or need a few nonsocial time to unwind and revive, at that point, the individual in question may not be a companion you need to keep close.

QUALITY OVER QUANTITY

Another negative part of living in a quick-paced world is the regular habit of attempting to fit more in a day than 24 hours can sensibly oblige. Occupied individuals need to do everything. They need to perform well at work, the sparkle in social settings, be great guardians, companions, or companions, and have a little personal time left at the day's end. While these are important objectives, fitting everything in each day may not be conceivable. Regardless of whether you do figure out how to plan everything, the time spent on every action might be constrained, surged, or, on the other hand, confounding. Instead, decide to do fewer things, however, do them well. Of endeavoring to go through two hours of family time each night, burn through four great hours on Saturday. Rather than saying yes each time a companion recommends an action, pick just those things that you will, as a matter of fact, appreciate together and that don't encroach on different commitments.

CLEAN UP YOUR MEDIA

At the point when you catch wind of cleaning up and association, media most likely never enters your thoughts. In all actuality, numerous individuals' lives are brimming with superfluous electronic media, for example, TV, long-range informal communication, and computer games. I am not one of those bad-to-the-bone people who need you to hurl out the big screen since TV decays your mind. In any case, I do think numerous individuals spend to an extreme degree an excess of time before a screen of some sort, and this can affect their whole life.

CLEAN UP TELEVISION HABITS

Consider how you sit in front of the TV. Are there times when you sit before the screen and watch whatever is on out of habit or inactivity? You are as of now there, so you check out the following program. There is a contrast between uninvolved TV seeing this way and watching a show you truly appreciate. There is an incentive to watching something that is engaging and contacts your heart or mind. Our family enjoys observing specific projects together in light of this. Here are a few things you can do to improve your TV habit so that you are watching programs you genuinely appreciate and removing regularly eating cushion.

Choose how much TV you can bear to watch every week.

Make a list of shows to watch and stop when you come to the designated time. This will drive you to organize. The record appears on a DVR or TiVo what's more, quick forward through advertisements to diminish the aggregate time spent on a show. Buy or lease appears on DVD to increment your family's authority over when and how you observe TV. Assign a specific time each evening for TV. Our family sits in front of the TV between 7:00 p.m. also, 9:00 p.m. on weeknights.

At the point when you start watching a show, assess how you or the family feel about it. Never continue observing an appearance since you began it. Your time is significant, and you need to fill it with amusement you genuinely appreciate.

CLEAN UP SOCIAL MEDIA HABITS

What number of online life accounts do you have, and how regularly do you check them? As an independent writer, I battled with time management for a while. I couldn't make sense of in what way numerous hours cruised by, yet I didn't get a lot of work done. As I checked out how I spent the time, I understood that I was routinely checking Facebook each time I utilized my program. I was not spending a lot of time during every session, except a couple of minutes were burnt through without fail. It presumably included through the span of a day to two hours or more.

CHECK OUT YOUR ONLINE NETWORKING HABITS.

You might be occupying your time with Twitter, Facebook, Tumblr, LinkedIn, and that's only the tip of the iceberg. Notwithstanding decreasing your efficiency, online networking use may include to your psychological mess. I found that when I read refreshes from various companions like clockwork, my psyche became busy with things other than the undertaking close by. From stress over wiped out companions to envy over somebody's most up to date excursion pictures, I was being occupied. Cleaning up your internet based life habits includes perceiving that they are an awful habit when you can do that, here are a few hints for keeping online networking associations without affecting your efficiency and mental focus.

Except if you need numerous accounts for business organizing purposes, pick a couple of social media accounts that you use routinely and where you can interface with the most companions. Abstain from enjoying, "friending" or following each individual you experience on the web. Keep your lists reasonable, and buy-in just to things you genuinely need to find out about every day.

Keep social media icons off your menu bars; there are apps such as "freezer" that you can use t hide them. If you need to type the address in, you are bound to consider what you are doing. Inquire about the web! Try not to utilize "keep me signed in" alternatives. Once more, Ify ou needs to type in your client name and password each time; you will acknowledge how much time you spend getting to online networking.

CONCLUSION

Anxiety is a thief of time and peace of mind. Every human will experience it at different times in life, as life would throw you a lot of challenges per time. The best way to live a happy life is to deal with it from its roots before it grows bigger than what you can handle. I hope this book has taught you a few practical ways to deal with anxiety, either in your home, offices, or simply protecting your mental health.

Now that you know these tips, the next step is to keep practicing them. You may want to pick up this book again and again, to read through some specific chapters just to remind yourself of how powerful you are against anxiety. Yes, you can live your best life, anxiety-free, and that time is NOW!